THE STORY OF THE SQUAMISH PEOPLE 1901-2022

Kultsia

ABSTRACT

A story of oral and written history of the Skwxwú7mesh people renamed in 1923 to the Squamish people. This account offers the peoples version from one family's research and preservation of oral and written history

wyss167@shaw.ca

Written by Kultsia Barbara Wyss
co-edited:
Sti7Hay SLan7ay Yvonne Wyss and
Dr T'uy't'tanat Cease Wyss

 iUniverse®

THE STORY OF THE SQUAMISH PEOPLE
1901-2022

iUniverse books may be ordered through booksellers or by contacting:

iUniverse
1663 Liberty Drive
Bloomington, IN 47403
www.iuniverse.com
844-349-9409

ISBN: 978-1-6632-3956-3 (sc)
ISBN: 978-1-6632-3957-0 (e)

Print information available on the last page.

iUniverse rev. date: 08/19/2022

A photo of Barbara with family members.

Book 4 – a story of the Skwxwú7mesh People, December 31, 2021

Contents

Abstract

My first three books, the Story of Skwxwú7mesh People, covered 1800 – 1900. This story began when most Skwxwú7mesh people permanently relocated to North Vancouver and were renamed the Squamish people by colonial government declaration in 1923.

This book covers the period from 1900 to 2021; The territory of the Skwxwú7mesh people was called New Caledonia, named by Britain. The British thought of lands with no British settlers to be unpopulated. A significant surge of people would begin arriving in New Caledonia, changing the lives of the Skwxwú7mesh people forever.

We are writing a story about the Skwxwú7mesh people's history. The unpacking and decolonizing of the research and dialogue have been recorded in the past 100-plus years since full colonial settlement.

The need to understand who the Skwxwú7mesh is to understand the people who have shaped and worked for the people. Many great Skwxwú7mesh leaders combined the new world of Canadian education through residential schools, and many also went back to the traditional teachings of Skwxwú7mesh elders. The following people are some who, in different ways, became leaders within the Skwxwú7mesh nation and some of their stories.

Joe Capilano   Joe Capilano SU-Á-PU-LUCK (Joseph Capilano) 1854 - 1910

Joe was born in the family of Letekwamcheten in a longhouse in Yekw'ts village in 1854. The large community was located on the Yookwitz Indian reserve Number 12 of the Skwxwú7mesh First Nation, on the right bank of the Skwxwú7mesh River, opposite the mouth of the Cheakamus River. There were two longhouses and several small buildings on the heavily forested land, which housed Joe and two other families. Letekwamchen and the other men hunted game meat and caught fish in the nearby rivers. The women tanned the hides and made clothing, woven mats, and baskets, mainly out of cedar bark, roots and boughs, and utilizing other natural materials such as stinging nettle fibres and cat tail rushes, to name a few. The elders raised the children while the parents did other work. This way of life had been occurring for thousands of years. Joe's father taught the boys to hunt and fish. He also spent time passing oral traditions of the daily life of the Skwxwú7mesh people. The oral passage of knowledge was how rituals, stories, ceremonies, skills, and education were shared with children.

a photo of Joe Capilano

Letekwamchen, Joe's father, told the stories of legends of Skwxwú7mesh Valley. He talked about how the mountain goats transformed into humans and visited people in one account. When Joe's parents died, he was a young man. After their death, Joe left his home in Yookowitz. Joe shared his knowledge with people through these stories. Joe moved to the Mission reserve in North Vancouver. Joe was a self-educated and robust man, earning the name Hiyas Joe. He gained skills in woodworking through sawmills and rail splitting at Moodyville. This work allowed him to hone his carving skills. Joe was strong enough to lift a long-handled axe with one hand and hold it straight out in front of him at the level of his shoulders, even well into his fifties.

Joe was a presence physically; he spoke and walked with the confidence of a man who was at his prime physically and as a head man among his people. His dark eyes were penetrating; people said he knew who they were when he gazed into a man. Joe never used alcohol or tobacco and shared his people's stories featuring homegrown humour; he always avoided profanity.

In Joe's visits around the Mission, he met Mary Agnes Lixwlut. She was the first-born daughter of Chief Skakhult; this marriage united two previously warring tribes, the Yuculta and the Skwxwú7mesh.

   Mary was the grand-niece of Old Chief Ki-ap-i-la-no; she was a beautiful woman with dark eyes and hair down to her middle; large deep, soft eyes stood out to Joe. Joe spoke to Mary's parents to announce his intentions to marry her. He agreed to be baptized in the church and married on the same day. Mary and Joe went on to have 12 children. She learned to be a genealogist in the new world approach to learning and teaching. Mary taught the children the Skwxwú7mesh language, culture, and pre-contact life. Mary lived for many years after Joe died of tuberculosis. She continued raising the children. She died in 1940. She taught each child about family ties, and they became fluent in the Skwxwú7mesh language by ten years of age. The kinship practice was oral within the Skwxwú7mesh People, passed down through the matrilineal lines. Mary told how her grandfather had met Captain George Vancouver upon his arrival on June 13, 1792, in Burrard Inlet.

Joe would often go climbing in the north shore mountains. He climbed the Ch'ichi-uy Twin Sisters, aka the Lions Mountains, to see the places of his stories. A mountain climbing group approached him as he carved a canoe one day. The fellow had heard that Joe could lead a group climbing the West Lion Mountain. In 1889, he guided a group of Englishmen on climbing the West Lion in North Vancouver. On another occasion, engineers needed help. They were part of a team to find a water source for Vancouver.

Joe spent time sitting with some Skwxwú7mesh carvers to learn how to carve. He wanted to develop his style of carving further. He began selling his carvings to Vancouver stores, and tourists were directed to his home.

In 1895, one of the leaders of the Skwxwú7mesh, Chief Lawa, drowned and did not leave an heir. Joe's wife Mary, the grandniece of Old Chief Ki-ap-ia-la-no, became the nearest relative. The church encouraged people to elect Su-a-pu-luck as chief. Bishop Durieux talked Joe into moving with some people to the Capilano reserve and built a church there. He spoke to people at the mission reserve and convinced them to construct a church on the Capilano Reserve.

Joe, like many Skwxwú7mesh men, found steady employment at Moodyville. Among the crews at Moodyville were Indian people from many different kinship families – including the Musqueam and Selílwitulh people around Vancouver. During their breaks, the workers would discuss many things, including political issues, such as Indian Rights, the land question, and the loss of resources.

Su-a-pu-luck spent his life in pursuit of the recognition of native rights. He would travel to other Indian tribes to encourage the quest for Aboriginal Rights.

Mary Capilano, sitting in her garden.

In 1906, when Joe was in London, he met Pauline Johnson (1861-1912), a famous Canadian poet. Her traditional name was Tekahionwake. She wrote nature poetry in the tradition of William Wordsworth. While waiting to meet the King, he spent some time with Pauline. She was fascinated with this group of BC Indian chiefs waiting to meet with the King. As a result of her meeting with Chief Joe Capilano, she came to Vancouver and spent much time with him and his wife. (Johnson, 1913) *The Legends of Vancouver* were told to her by Chief Joe Capilano and his wife.

 Joe died in 1910 of tuberculosis. Mary survived him by 30 years. She became widely known for her talents as a basket weaver to support the family. Even in her older years, she often paddled her dugout canoe to cross the First Narrows between the Capilano Reserve and downtown Vancouver. Mary would live long enough to witness the devastating effects of the Indian Act and the resulting theft of Skwxwú7mesh land.

Chief August Jack, Khahsalano - Xats'alanexw. 1871 - 1971, in St. Paul's Hospital, Vancouver.

Jack was born in Chaythoos, Stanley Park, in 1877, in Vancouver, BC. Jack's parents were Khay-Tulk and Quay-wat. When he was a little boy, his father, Kha y-Tulk, died from a brain injury resulting from a kick in the head from a cow. His mother remarried a man known as Jericho Charlie. His grandfather was hereditary Chief Xats'alanexw. Chief August, Jack Khahsalano was also known as a Skwxwú7mesh Medicine Man for his detailed and unmatched knowledge of his local medicines and plants.

In 1879, his parents brought him to a priest for baptism. Unfortunately, Father N. Gregane recorded the incorrect information. In 1946, August had the baptismal information corrected at the Vancouver City Archives.

August Jack, 6' tall, had a strong, straight back. He had a broad face, with large brown spots sprinkled around his face. His voice was strong, deep, and forceful. Jack had a straight back in his younger years, but it became bent slightly from leaning forward from years of heavy work and carving.

August shared over 22 years of interviews with Major Matthews, the city of Vancouver's archivist. This would produce the *Journals of August Jack Khahtsalano*. One such story:

One day, while the family was having a meal, city workers started to build a road right through their house. There had been no warning or written notice that a road would be going right through their home. The workers just showed up with a bulldozer and work crew. What they were doing was installing Stanley Park Road. August buried his father near their home in Stanley Park. Fortunately, the family could remove his father's casket and bring it to Xwemélch'stn Village, [a Skwxwú7mesh village site by the Capilano River], where their family graveyard sat above Swey'wey Creek. The work crew destroyed August's house at Chaythoos, and the family moved to Snauq, where he lived for most of his early life. His early years were divided between Chaythoos (near Brockton Oval) and Snauq' because his father owned the two houses, so they moved back and forth between the two houses. Snauq' is where they lived until 1913. (Matthews,1955).

In 1900, August and his brother Willie worked in a sawmill at Falsecreek to save money to host a naming ceremony. The ceremony celebrated August Jack taking Xats'alanexw [Khahtsalano], his grandfather's name. The ceremony, observed in the longhouse of Toe-wyo-Quam-kee at the village of Snauq', attracted many visitors. Guests came from xʷməθkwəy̓əm [Musqueam], Snu'nuy'mexw [Nanaimo], Sechelt, and Sla7an Village as well. From then on, August became known as August Jack Xats'alanexw or Khahtsalano, as Major Mathews had written his name. Other spellings of his grandfather's name include Kates-ee-lan-ogh and 'Haatslano".

August Jack and his wife Mary Ann (Swanamia) lived with their children in Snauq until 1913, leaving the reserve land. The Vancouver Harbor Commission forced the families of Snauq' to go and cross to the Capilano reserve and the Mission reserve in a barge. Colonial settlers' demand for land removed the families, and their homes burned behind them as the families were barged out into the harbour. The land would not be returned to the People until 1996 in a landmark case that would produce only 10.4 acres of land back and a cash settlement of over 92.6 million dollars. The Squamish Nation holds trust over the Xats'alanexw [Khahtsalano] family and their descendants.

This picture shows a barge with people on it. In 1913, the B.C. government under Conservative premier Richard McBride forced the Skwxwú7mesh people to abandon their homes so Vancouver could expand. (Indigenous Foundations/UBC)

Mary Ann is a beautiful woman with a high forehead, a long nose, a pointed chin, and delicate brows. She was very lively and had great strength. She would barbecue salmon on an open fire. The work required selecting the salmon, preparing it, and using (ocean spray or ironwood sticks) (to secure it for cooking on an open fire, harvesting the Wood that doesn't burn to cook the salmon. (T'uy't'tanat Cease Wyss, Knowledge Keepers: Medicine Walk 2020, p. 13)

After a few years, the family moved to a Skwxwú7mesh reserve near a sawmill. His work included bringing logs down the Skwxwú7mesh River to the mill. August built canoes and created totem poles when he was not at the mill.

Major James Skitt Matthews (7 September 1878 – 1 October 1970) was Vancouver's first archivist and an early historian and chronicler. Matthews enjoyed meeting with Aboriginal people as well as the colonialists of Vancouver. So, when he met Chief August Jack, he was excited to meet someone knowledgeable about local Indian history.

Matthews would meet with August whenever he came to the archaeologist's office. From 1932 to 1954, Major Matthews recorded August Jack's stories and personal history. Jack became an indispensable resource in providing some of the narratives of the Skwxwú7mesh Nation. Major Mathews published a book about his many conversations with August, called, (Matthews, 1955)

Conversations with August Jack, 1932-1954.

(Mathews, J. 1955. "Conversations with Khahtsalano." Vancouver, BC. Mathews, Major. City of Vancouver Archives-Major Matthews Early Vancouver

Chief Khahtsalano.

Chief Louis Miranda 1892 - 1990

Louis Miranda was born in 1892 to Cecilia, a Skwxwú7mesh band member and his father, Frank Miranda, had immigrated from Chile. Frank went to work at Moodyville Mill. He met many Skwxwú7mesh people there and visited Sla7an Village during his time off work. During his visits, he met Cecilia. They were married in the Mission church. When Louis was born, the parents had a naming ceremony for him at home. Cecilia called for witnesses, and a Skwxwú7mesh chief gave Louis the hereditary name of Sxaaltwx. Unfortunately, his father died when Louis was 12 years old. Although the Chilean government offered to transport him to Chile to live with surviving members of the Miranda family, Cecilia chose to keep Louis with her and raise him herself at the Mission reserve.

Cecilia's family originally came from the Skwxwú7mesh Chewelp Indian Reserve, located on the west side of Keats Island in Howe Sound, BC. She took him to his home reserve when he was a young man familiar with the place. They spent three weeks at Chewelp before returning to the Mission reserve/Sla7an Village. She also taught him the language, culture, history, and way of life. Cecilia also taught Louie many stories and legends.

On his mother's side, Louis was a descendent of a chief at Chewelp. When the headman at Chewelp died, Louis inherited the ancestral title. Louis's family at Chewelp village and Schenks are talked about in Skwxwú7mesh oral history as the birthplace of the Skwxwú7mesh people after what they call the great flood.

Louis stood 5'10" tall; dark-skinned, with bushy eyebrows, high cheekbones, sagging skin below the eyes, a long thin mouth, dark eyes, and thick eyebrows. His wrinkles showed the wisdom of his years as a provider of information about the Skwxwú7mesh people. He was of medium weight, with a bent back. His voice was strong, gentle, and warm. He was married to Jessie.

For 53 years, Louis met with many people. Before the 1960s, the Skwxwú7mesh people did not have a written language. Louis felt strongly that the language was in peril and worked with linguists from several institutions to develop a written system. Fortunately, Aert Hendrik Kuipers (10/11/1919-1/-1/12/2012), a Dutch linguistics professor, worked with Louis during the 1950s to compile the first detailed reference grammars of Skwxwú7mesh Snichem [Squamish Language]. (Aert Kuipers - Bing). Together, they gathered a two-volume work called The

Skwxwú7mesh Language, published in 1967-68 by Aert Kuipers. This system has remained adopted as the official written language of the Skwxwú7mesh Nation.

A Picture of Dominic Charlie, Louis Miranda and his wife Jessie sitting with a crowd.

Louis worked with Randy Bouchard, Dorothy Kennedy and Nancy Turner on research conducted during the 1960-1980s. They collected information on the Skwxwú7mesh Nation's close connection to the land, water, and air in their defined territory, from which they developed an intricate culture, government, and economy. (Reimer, 2003)

As a result of Louis's work with Randy Bouchard and Dorothy Kennedy, a book on Skwxwú7mesh plants and Skwxwú7mesh legends was produced.

Andrew Paull   Xwechtáal, Xwupúkinem, Quitchtaal) (February 6, 1892 – July 28, 1959)

Andrew was born to Dan Paull and Theresa Paull [nee Lacket-Joe] in 1892. They were a high-standing family who lived in a longhouse in Sta7amus, BC. Several families shared the longhouse, which included Andy's grandparents. While the family lived there, his grandmother gave him the ancestral name of Xwechtáal [which refers to the Serpent Slayer, as told in our creation stories].

Andy's parents moved to Sla7an Village, North Vancouver, in the late 1800s. His father became employed at Moodyville. While Andy and his family lived at the Mission, the Bishop began the

Durieux System. The system controlled the people who lived in cruel and terrible ways at the Mission reserve. (Gresko, 1990)

Early in Paull's school career, the literary instincts, which had always been present in him, came from his mother. His mother had helped him develop his literary works by inspiring him through her restless imaginative ways of approaching life, and the world made itself feel those words with considerable force.

He did not know English when he entered school at seven. He learned English from French-speaking nuns. His teachers would give him the tools to be a successful writer, speaker, and political organizer. For the rest of his life, Andy credited his successful learning experiences to his time at the school.

After six years at residential school, Andy spent two years learning from Skwxwú7mesh elders who lived at the Mission. He would invite the elders to come to his home. His mother would provide tea, sandwiches, and a variety of cakes. After the afternoon of teachings, Andy would give elders a thank-you to recognize their time teaching him. The elders sensed in Andy an excellent future for improving the living conditions of the Skwxwú7mesh people. He learned about the people, history, way of life, customs, language, and culture.

He was ready to learn about Canadian law. Andy asked many people about finding a law firm. Finally, Andy asked the priest for help in locating a law firm. The priest then asked the Archbishop of Vancouver for help in Andy's search. Andy's search led him to Hugh St. Quentin.

In 1907, he began work at the law firm of Hugh St. Quentin Cayley. Hugh was a lawyer, newspaper reporter/owner and politician. Mr. Cayley took a great interest in Andrew Paull. Therefore, he included Andrew's legal teachings and newspaper reporting. Furthermore, Mr. Cayley taught Andy the basics of being a Politician. His suggestions included listening to the people's concerns and proposing changes in laws that relate to the needs of the people. In addition, he encouraged Andy to make public appearances at various political functions and events. Cayley has a vast law library and access to the law library at UBC. Andy thanked his mother for developing the desire to read because he learned that he would need to read many books to attain a law degree. When he reached the time to receive a law degree, Andy had to make a life-changing decision. He had reached the point of acquiring a law degree; at that time, the Indian Affairs rule was that Indian people had to give up their Indian status if they received a university degree. In later years, he would represent the Indian people in court. Andy could speak for them in their defence, but he did not have a law degree. He left the law firm and went as a labourer at Moodyville Sawmill, located a few blocks east of Lonsdale Street, North Vancouver. Over time, Andy tried many other types of work and occupations. Andy also worked part-time as a secretary to Chief Harry of Sla7an.

He stood about 5'10" tall; his back was ramrod straight and had the physical bearing of an athlete prepared for running in the Olympics. He had a deep dimple on his cheeks that always seemed ready to smile. He wore his hair in a crew-cut style and had short eyebrows that angled upwards. Andy's eyes were very dark. He had a high forehead, a sign of someone who had incredible intellect. His voice was strong, deep, and loud, evident when he spoke in meetings and gatherings. When Andy stood at the microphone and looked at his parliamentarians' audience, he sternly gazed at them. But then he smiled as he began his speech and spoke at length in a casual voice. Andrew Paull married Josephine Joseph (nee Lacket-Joe) in 1914, and they had seven children. Josephine was described as very sweet, kind, thoughtful and caring. She loved animals and was very kind to people with special needs. Their children's names were Audrey (Frank Rivers), Percy (Georgina), Yvonne (Willard), Helen (Dale George), Marian, Evelyn, and Edna.

Andy was also a labour organizer, working to organize hop-pickers in the Fraser Valley and later organizing a new organization, the Native Brotherhood of BC. Another side to his life involved helping Aboriginal music bands, training, and booking their concerts, starting with the Skwxwú7mesh people. He chose Jim Nahanee, Frank Rivers, Harold Natrall, Charlie Joe, James John, and Vern Billy. They learned to play many instruments and played at dances, weddings, and concerts. When Andy could, he organized sports activities.

Chief Dan George Born 1899 - September 23, 1982

Chief Geswanouth Dan George [Sla-holt]. Dan was born on July 24, 1899. to Sla-holt [James George and Annie Harry George. Annie was an intellectual woman and had excellence in everything except sports. Annie taught Dan the gift of music. She taught him Skwxwú7mesh songs using drums. But unfortunately, she stopped when he entered the residential school.

Annie worked with the mothers of the children that were taken away and sent to the residential school. She helped them develop sewing circles to fill their loneliness of empty homes. She also played an instrumental role in founding the Burrard Indian Women's Social Club. It provided a forum for discussing the day's issues for both men and women. She worked with young people to increase their awareness of the world outside the community they lived in.

Dan lived at the Mission reserve when he left the school. He attended parties and socials with his friends from school. At one of the parties, he met a young woman named Amy. Amy's parents were Chief Henry Jack and Christine Jack.

Dan started residential school at the age of five. The priests forced Dan to change his name to Dan George because the catholic church wanted the Skwxwú7mesh people to have only Anglican first names. Dan had many friends as a youth with a natural gift of sympathy. He loved field hockey and often participated in his youth.

He had his mother's delight in living. He loved field hockey and canoeing; his athletic instincts and his athletic friends always fought in him with his literary instincts. The rule at the school was that when the student reached the age of 16, they were to leave the school. Dan had to pursue employment. Two pursuits Dan continued were a love of music and entertaining people. In Dan, all the time, there was a strength of will, a force and even tyranny of conscience, which kept his charm and compliancy from degenerating into weakness and made it delightful to love him. He honoured his mother, a life-giver, as his driving force in life.

When Dan left school, he worked as a longshoreman at Moodyville in North Vancouver and later at a sawmill at Burrard, construction worker, and school bus driver. From 1951 to 1963, Dan became the Chief of what was then known as the Burrard Indian Band. Chief Dan George was married to Amy George in 1918, and for 51 years, they would have ten children: Betty, Robert, Winona, Susan, Rose, Jesse, Amy Marie, Ann, Rose, and Leonard. He had many grandchildren and many great-grandchildren.

Dan spent many years meeting with his elders to learn the way of life of his people and songs and legends. Then, Dan began to make appearances at many concerts and events with his children, who sang and performed songs and dances, both modern and traditional. Their Group was known as "The Children of Takaya," and it continues today through their descendants.

During this time, he caught the attention of television producers looking for authentic Indian actors. In Hollywood, he was nominated as a supporting actor in the film "Little Big Man." He was "a role model for many people, too many to name. Dan helped change the popular image of Indigenous people, often misrepresented in negative and stereotypical ways.

Dan was 5'10" tall and had shoulder-length hair, a weather-beaten face that was deeply wrinkled, showing the wisdom of a long life, and a wide mouth, a prominent nose, and thick bushy eyebrows. Dan's smile had little wrinkles around his eyes. Dan had a straight back, like a warrior of old, someone who protected his people in peace and war. He was slender, strong, and defiant when he was about to make an important statement, with a look of boldness at the world around him.

One of his most publicized presentations was called "Lament for Confederation." It was a prose poem about the oppression and resurgence of Indigenous peoples in Canada. Chief Dan George asks the settler-colonialists:

"Oh Canada, how can I celebrate with you this centenary, this hundred year?

But, first, shall I thank you for the reserves left me of my beautiful forests?

Shall I thank you for the canned fish of my rivers?

Shall I thank you for the loss of my pride and authority, even among my people?

For the lack of my will to fight back,

No! I must forget what is past and gone."

(McCardle, 2007)

This monologue, an indictment of European colonialism's appropriation of native territory, was performed at the City of Vancouver's celebration of the Canadian centennial in 1967. Dan always encouraged Indigenous people to become self-empowered in the colonial society imposed on them.

Dan George wrote various books and poems during his career, of which his best-written book is called "My Heart Soars" (1974) -- a collection of poetry and prose.

Dan George died at Lions Gate Hospital at the age of 82.

Skwxwú7mesh women

Indigenous women are strong. They maintain their homes. They taught their children and grandchildren their language, culture, and way of life and supported their husbands. Here is the story of a Skwxwú7mesh woman.

The role of Skwxwú7mesh women: the act of genocide practiced on Indian women, from the earliest dates of the Indian Act coming into effect in 1876 and lasting until significant changes to Government Legislation in 1985. The Indigenous Women of Canada succeeded in making a substantial change to the Act. This would open a catalyst for more changes to correct the wrongs of the Act. The fight began in 1970 during the battle for indigenous women's rights when Jeannette Corbiere Laval took Canada to court because Canada violated the 1960 Bill of Rights. After all, it discriminated against her based on sex. She lost the case. She appealed the decision. Another woman, Yvonne Bedard, also went to court. The National Indian Brotherhood fought against the women and called the women anti-Indian because they viewed the Indian Act as guaranteeing the right of Indian self-determination. On August 27, 1973, the Supreme of Canada stated that the Bill of Rights did not invalidate the Indian Act and Jeannette lost her case.

This would open the door for Indigenous people to fight for rights legally. The changes for women worldwide began with the fight for equal opportunities and greater personal freedoms. This fight would take until 1985 when the women would regain their rights. Finally, in 1985, the Parliament of Canada changed the Indian Act to end some sections that discriminated against Indian women and children.

Teressa Ann Nahanee. 1946-2022

Teressa is the fourth child of Lorne Whitten and Eva May Nahanee. When she was five years old, Teressa, her older sister Barbara, and her younger siblings Roberta, Lorne, and Jason were put into St. Paul's Indian residential school. Indian Affairs Indian Act stated that children between the age of seven and 16 were required to be put into a residential school. In some cases, such as Lorne Nahanee, the children were three years old and older. They would remain there for five years. Teressa attended St. Paul's school as a day student until she reached grade eight. Then she attended St. Thomas Aquinas until she graduated grade 12.

Teressa listened to her dad say Barbara would become a lawyer with her other siblings. This was like a challenge to her. She wanted to prove that she would become the first lawyer in the family. In her teenage years, Teressa and her siblings went to Washington State to pick strawberries and to Yarrow, BC, for raspberries. They stayed at the farm for two weeks of the season. Her summer was also spent working in the fish cannery. Because she was a high school graduate, she got to work in the office. Auntie Effie always brought lots of food for lunch. [She wanted her nieces to become heavy-set like her]. She did go to university and graduated from Notre Dame University in Nelson, BC. Her mom and some brothers and sisters were able to attend her graduation ceremony. Barbara was working at the Vancouver Friendship Center at the time. Teressa came there and sent out some newsletters. Mom took Teressa to Indian Affairs to discuss her future. She told the department, "Well, you said she should get educated; now, get her a job." The department found her work in their newsletter department, but it was in Ottawa. It meant she had to move thousands of miles from the family home. While in Ottawa, she attended the University of Ottawa. She studied English and Law. Furthermore, Teressa obtained a master's degree from Queens University, Kingston.

While at Indian Affairs, the general rule was that the Indian employees were kept at lower-level jobs. However, one of her managers helped her move to a management-level position. Teressa wrote and published a newsletter in her department. She had to pick up the newsletter in Montreal and then return it to her office to have it mailed across Canada.

Teressa cared for two young children she raised independently from a previous relationship. She decided to teach them to play poker. She did this and enjoyed looking after the children. Her other joy was taking her mother on holidays. She brought her mom to Ottawa for a holiday. It included taking her mom to Montreal to visit Saint Joseph's Oratory of Mount Royal (French: Oratoire Saint-Joseph du Mont-Royal), a Roman Catholic minor basilica and national shrine on Mount Royal's Westmount Summit in Montreal, Quebec. It is Canada's largest church and claims to have one of the giant domes in the world. Our mom walked up the stairs, a very long walk up the steps. The last trip Teressa brought our mom on was to Trinidad in 1977. Our mom passed away on that trip. Teressa was able to get permission to have our mom's body brought back to North Vancouver to bury her near dad's grave. We had a traditional burning for her. Our mother worked hard to teach us traditional ways, but it was difficult because the government forced our parents to put us in residential school. Our hands were up to Teressa for taking our mom on holiday trips.

Teressa worked with the Native Women's Association of Canada. This is where she met Sharon McIvor, and they worked together on the issue of Indian Rights for Indian Women. Sharon is Teressa's Life partner. And together, they helped thousands of indigenous people to return to their communities.

In 1979, Teressa heard that a group of Tobique women organized by Caroline Ennis, a student at St. Thomas University, Fredericton, NB, had organized a march to Ottawa to protest discrimination in the Indian Act against women. Teressa went to Montreal to join the walk. She rented a car and drove some of the older women marching. She rented a room at night so the women could sleep in a comfortable space. When the walk was completed in Ottawa, she wrote a report of the event. It received worldwide attention about the treatment of Indigenous women. Indian Affairs was not pleased.

Women from BC to the Atlantic coast mobilized a series of speaking and writing campaigns across Canada to raise the profile of abuses faced by women who had been denied status, treaty, and property rights under the *Indian Act*. The women's walk from Tobique reached the United Nations Human Rights Commission and censored Canada.

Section 35 of the Constitution Act, 1982 was not included in Prime Minister Pierre Trudeau's initial proposal for patriation in 1980. Aboriginal Canadians had not been consulted about the new constitution, and there was initially a minimal reference to Aboriginal rights. Aboriginal groups across Canada became concerned that, with the transfer of constitutional powers from Britain to Canada, established agreements affirming Aboriginal rights and title would no longer hold legal weight. Aboriginal groups were also concerned that they would no longer be viewed as autonomous decision-makers on a federal level. They saw the potential for the patriation to be yet another assimilationist policy, much like the 1969 White Paper, also proposed by the Trudeau government.

It took two years and raising concerns before an international audience, including the United Nations and the British Parliament, before the Canadian government finally agreed to include

Aboriginal rights in the constitution. Because of Canada's Aboriginal peoples' intense fight for recognition, Section 35 was added to the Constitution in time to be formally patriated in 1982. Section 35 initially consisted of clauses (1) and (2). Clauses (3) and (4) section was further developed in 1983-4 because of consultations with Aboriginal representatives during the First Ministers' Conference on Aboriginal Rights in March 1983. After lengthy campaigns, these clauses were added by women's groups, who were unrepresented in the initial discussions and experienced systemic gender discrimination.

Indigenous women fought extensively to be included in the constitutional discussions, especially with the Indigenous men's groups. Teressa Nahanee and Sharon McIvor worked with the Native Women's Association of Canada to represent the talks. They were harassed, insulted, humiliated, and sexually assaulted because they wanted women's rights included. They brought their case to court. Finally, Indigenous women were allowed a seat. Canada granted funds, but the money was distributed to the men's groups. The men's group said, OK, here is $5,000. Teressa then told her brother, Rennie, we have $5000; can you create something with this. He created a video for her, which was broadcast across Canada. Sharon and Teressa made it work. This video was a rarity in the Opposition of the Charlottetown Accord; it would get played against every yes video created and gained immense popularity. The Accord would die. (McIvor, 2021)

NWAC's fight to secure equal funding from the Government of Canada to participate in the Canada Round of constitutional discussions:

In summary, in 1994, the Supreme Court of Canada (SCC) ruled against the claimants in Native Women's Association of Canada v. Canada. The SCC ruled that the **Canadian Charter of Rights and Freedoms had not been violated by the federal government's decision not to include NWAC in constitutional debates**. (Native Women's Association of Canada vs Canada, 1982)

In 1984, Teressa became Special Assistant to David Crombie, Minister of Indian Affairs. As part of her duties, she helped the minister write changes to the Indian Act. In 1985, Parliament passed Bill C-31. Bill C-31 was used to amend the Indian Act to conform with the equality rights guaranteed by s.15 of the Canadian Charter of Rights and Freedoms (Charter). When introduced, the amendments were neutral concerning a person's gender or marital status. The amendments allowed women who previously lost their Indian Status to regain their children's Indian status.

In addition, after Bill C-31 was adopted, a person's marriage could no longer affect their receiving or losing Indian status. Bill C-31 brought about several changes, such as Indian women, who married a non-Indian man, no longer lost their Indian status; Indian women, who previously lost their Indian status because of their marriage to non-Indian men, were allowed to apply to have their Indian status returned to them. Their children were also given the same right. Non-Indian women could no longer gain Indian status by marrying Indian men; non-Indian women, who got their Indian status through marriage before 1985, did not lose their status. The process of enfranchisement was removed entirely. In addition, the Indian Registrar could no longer remove those people from the Indian Register who had the right to registration. Individuals who were voluntarily or involuntarily enfranchised under the Indian Act before we're allowed to apply for the return of their Indian status. The federal government continued to have control over Indian registration. Also, new categories of registered Indians were created in the Indian Act through sections 6(1) and 6(2).

Teressa was a matriarch who stood for the rights of Indigenous women and dedicated her life's work to improve indigenous women's situations across Turtle Island [the Indigenous name for North America].

[Barbara on the left], Teressa [holding her degree], and Sharon McIvor [beside Teressa], these three women were part of many Indigenous women across Canada to fight for the changes to the Indian Act.

Lena Jacobs nee Band 9 February 1910 - 2008

Lena was 98 years old when she passed. Lena was born on the Mission Reserve IR No. 1 in North Vancouver, BC [AKA Sla7an Village], on February 9, 1910. She was the daughter of the late George Joseph Band & Marie-Anne "Molly" Baker. Lena proudly shared 50+ years with her late husband, Alfred Isaac Jacob. Her children who survived her: Russell Alfred Isaac Jacobs Sr.; George Peter Jacobs Sr. (Christine); Sharon Olive Mary Schoerneck (Hart Sr.); Chief Gilbert "Gibby" Joseph Jacob (Vivian). Son-In-Law: Don Willie. She has 29 grandchildren, 67 great-grandchildren, and 11 great-great-grandchildren. Many loving relatives and dear friends. Early in her life, Lena worked at the Great Northern Cannery in West Vancouver and Canadian Fisheries on the Foot of Gore Street in Vancouver.

Lena was one of the few fluent speakers of the Skwxwú7mesh Nation language. Her legacy will continue through her teachings and values of the culture and language of her people; she has instilled this practice in her children and grandchildren to carry on for generations. Will Lena be remembered for her active role with the Skwxwú7mesh Nation's Wa Chexw Nexwni? wn t an I? mats. Most certainly! One of Lena's Grandchildren is Peter Jacobs, who works in the Skwxwú7mesh Nation language department. She was a devout Christian, full of grace and elegance, and possessed a strong constitution and a warm demeanour that embraced and greeted all.

Audrey Rivers 1930-2018

Audrey Rivers descends from the Andrew Paull/Charlie and Joseph/Moses Families. She was born in Vancouver on Dec. 2, 1930, and is predeceased by her parents, Andrew Paull Xwupúkinem-t and Josephine Paull, husband Frank Rivers Sr; siblings Percy Paull- Xwechtaal-t, Yvonne Paull- Sxananalh-t, Josephine 'Hudo' Lauridsen, Edna Paull, Marion Paull, and Evelyn Paull, and children Irene 'Linda' Rivers, and Frank Rivers Jr. She passed surrounded by family on September 7, 2018, in North Vancouver at Lions Gate Hospital. She was 87 years young. Audrey grew up beside St. Paul's Catholic Church on Mission Reserve IR# 1. Audrey and her husband lived close to where she was born. She went to St. Paul's Residential School and attended Sprott

Shaw College. Audrey was married to Frank for over 25 years. Audrey worked as an administrator for her father in a legal firm and then the Mosquito Creek Marina. She spent many years on the Membership and Skwxwú7mesh Language Advisory Committees. Audrey carried the Olympic torch over Burrard Street Bridge with Rick Hansen and did the opening prayer for the 2010 Special Olympics. Audrey spoke Skwxwú7mesh Language fluently and was often asked to do opening and closing prayers for events. She was part of the International Choir and the 'God Squad.' Audrey is survived by her Children Lillian Rivers, Glenn Rivers (Linda), Donna Joseph (nee Dick), Kevin Rivers, Sheryl Rivers, Grandchildren Trevor Rivers, Jill Peters, Kim Wilson, nee Peters (Doug), Julie Peters, Darryl Douglas, Lily Rivers, Delmar Williams, Temora Williams Miller (Wylie), Melanie Rivers (Aaron), Travis Billy, Courtney Dick, Joshua Anderson (Karmen), Amanda Anderson, Josie Joseph, Kristen Rivers (Karen), Dustin Rivers, many Great Grandchildren, and Great-Great Grandchildren.

Mazie Baker 1931 - 2011

Mazie is a matriarch and an elder. She was born to Sarah and Moses Antone in 1931 on the Mission Reserve, North Vancouver. Her parents, Moses and Sarah Antone, were hard-working people who loved their families. When Ms. Johnson, the author of *the Amazing Mazie Baker,* first met Mazie Baker, she knew her as the reigning queen of Bannock, selling out batch after batch of fluffy, light frybread at local powwows. She soon learned that Mazie, a matriarch, and activist, had been nurturing and fiercely protecting her community for a lifetime. In 1931, Mazie Antone was born into the Skwxwú7mesh Nation, a society caught between its traditional values of respect for the land, the family and the band and the secular, capitalistic legislation imposed by European settlers. When she was six, the police carried her off to St. Paul's Indian Residential School, as mandated by the 1920 Indian Act. She endured months of beatings, malnourishment and lice infestations before her family collected Mazie and her siblings and fled to Washington State, in the United States. They stayed in Washington for years because the parents faced going to jail for years returned while the children were of school age. This was the Indian Act law of 1920.

Once in Washington, the Antones weathered the Depression by picking fruit and working in the shipyards. After the war, the children were old enough to safely return to their home on the

Capilano Reserve. At sixteen, Mazie began working at a fish cannery; she worked in fish canneries for eleven years, learning to defend herself from supervisors and fellow packers foolish enough to make her a target. Mazie married her sweetheart, Alvie Baker, and they raised nine children together. Part of the legacy of residential school was that Mazie and her generation were alienated from their culture and language, but through her children, she reconnected with her Skwxwú7mesh identity. She came to mourn the loss of the old style of government by councils of hereditary chiefs and to criticize the corruption in the band leadership created in 1981 by Skwxwú7mesh band members. This process was monitored by Indian Affairs, which gave federal approval. She began a long advocacy career, galvanized by the injustices she saw against and within her community, especially against indigenous women, who were denied status and property rights. She attended every council meeting and general meeting. She challenged those in power, including where the money was going. Not only did Mazie attend band council meetings, but she was also invited to Ottawa to appear before Parliamentary meetings. In her community, she fought for housing for needy families; she pushed for transparency in local government, defended ancestral lands, and shone a bright light into the darkest political corners. For instance, a family member's land was taken from him, and she fought for him. Her family called her chicken: Golden Eagle. Kay Johnson has written a fascinating biography of a beautiful, feisty principled woman. This intimate biography of a community leader illuminates a problematic, unresolved chapter of Canadian history and paints a portrait of a resilient and honest woman who faced her every political foe, unflinching, irreverent, and uncompromising. Mazie died fighting for the people at a general meeting.

"With empathy, compassion and a keen eye for the hard facts, Kay Johnston has crafted the definitive biography of Mazie Baker, a true champion for human rights who has been overlooked in the history books of Canada. This insightful narrative gives us a glimpse into the woman and the warrior who crusaded for justice and a brighter way forward for all First Nations peoples.

" "The Amazing Mazie Baker" contributes to the growing record of Indigenous peoples telling stories of resistance, resilience, and resurgence. The book will interest those studying women's and gender history, Indigenous feminisms, and political organizing in colonial contexts." Sean Carleton, BC Studies

"From her days as a cannery worker to her appearance before the Senate Standing Committee on Aboriginal Peoples in 1999, while raising children, nurturing grandchildren, and providing sound counsel to many Band members, this book provides a vivid portrait of an inspiring resilient woman, one whose voice continues to echo." Theresa Kishkan, Author of *Patrin* and A Man in a Distant Field

Cecilia Nahanee. 1880-1918

She was the first wife of William Nahanee. Cecilia Johnny (1880-1918) was the daughter of Lacey and Johnny, granddaughter of X'alek and great-granddaughter of Khahtsalano. Cecilia lived on the Mission reserve before her marriage to William Nahanee. When they married, Cecilia and William moved to Moodyville, a huge sawmill and onshore community. Moodyville was a community made up mainly of Kanakas. It was the so-called "Kanaka Row" because many Hawaiians lived there. William's father was a Hawaiian living at the Kanaka Ranch, Stanley Park, Vancouver.

William met Cecilia, and they courted for a short time. They married, and they had eight children. Unfortunately, their oldest son, Joe, only lived for a year. Joe's grave is at the cemetery in West Vancouver Indian Reserve.

Cecilia had another son, and her mother was happy to learn the news. In ancient times, a baby boy had a board tied to the baby's forehead. The reason to do this was to flatten the forehead and change the shape of their head to a flat, elongated profile. The Indian people believed that this was a sign of superior intelligence. Granny Lacey wanted Cecilia to do this to Edward. However, Cecilia refused the request. Cecilia was a devout Christian who did not want to use ancient practices.

Although she only lived a mile from her childhood home, Cecilia was lonesome for her siblings and other family members. To get to Sla7an, Cecilia walked a wide trail along the shoreline. Sometimes, Cecilia paddled a canoe to Sla7an. William loved Cecilia and was concerned for her. Therefore, he arranged to move the family to Sla7an.

Maude, the oldest daughter, recalled that her mother had Tuberculosis or consumption. This illness started after a great epidemic almost wiped out the people on the Mission reserve. Cecilia had some training as a nurse. The training helped Cecilia organize workers to attend to the sick and dying. The sickness was the result of the Spanish Flu. The Spanish Flu pandemic killed 30 to 50 million people worldwide. In the Mission reservation, many people died. People were starting to recover. However, Cecilia became weakened from her long hours of work. She had used all her energy nursing the people and had little energy for herself. The doctor told her family that Cecilia would linger for a long time. Cecilia's daughter Maude could have gone to Tranquille Hospital to study to be a nurse, she didn't want to go so far from home and needed to care for her mother. Home care meant that everything was kept very sanitary at home. Cecilia's bedding and dishes had to be kept separate from other family members. Cecilia's laundry needed individual cleaning. Maude arranged for a laundry service.

We know from Maude that Cecilia was a very religious woman. Her daughter, Maude, read all the stories of the saints to her. Cecilia's illness worsened, and the VON nurse would visit every day. Cecilia continued to care for and worry about her children throughout her illness. She was concerned about Maude, her oldest daughter. Cecilia encouraged Maude to get on with her life and get married.

Cecilia enjoyed helping at the church with cleaning and bringing flowers for the altar. In addition, Cecilia would spend time teaching the community ladies to bake cakes and crochet. Unfortunately, Cecilia could no longer do all this when she became ill. Cecilia died in 1918. Cecilia and William taught their children the Skwxwú7mesh language, customs, and traditions. Unfortunately, the catholic nuns stopped these teachings. The parents enrolled the children at the residential school. The teachers pressured students not to speak their language, follow their traditional ways, and become devout Christians. Many parents at Sla7an did not feel that education was important. Some parents did see the importance of education and had their children educated for as many years as possible. In those days, the students stayed in school until they were 16, then they had to leave school.

In 1906-07, William took his eldest son, Edward, into Vancouver to purchase a heavy bag and gloves. He taught his son pugilistic skills. In 1924, his younger son, William Jr., would enter boxing tournaments held in the hop fields of the Fraser Valley. From 1946-to 1960, seven of William's grandsons belonged to the Totem Athletic Boxing Club. Many of William's sons, grandsons, and nephews became boxers. Sla7an had facilities for indoor sports. Tournaments were held at the auditorium and elsewhere. The Nahanee boys were thrilled to meet Jim

Thorpe, American Indian "Bright Path," an American Indian athlete and Olympic gold medalist in 1953. Jim Thorpe had heard about the boxing club in North Vancouver.

A Sac and Fox Nation member, Thorpe became the first Native American to win a gold medal for the United States. Considered to be one of the most versatile athletes of modern sports, he won Olympic gold medals in the 1912 pentathlon and decathlon. Jim played American football (collegiate and professional), professional baseball, and basketball. A terrible injustice happened to Jim Thorpe. He was found guilty of being paid as a professional sports player. As a result, Jim lost his Olympic titles. A committee informed Jim that he violated the amateurism rules in place. In 1983, 30 years after his death, the International Olympic Committee restored his Olympic medals. In 1952, Jim Thorpe watched one of the Buckskin Gloves tournaments where boxers at St. Paul's Indian Residential were boxing.

Lorne, William's youngest son, recalled an interesting family legend about the Nahanni River inland from the northern British Columbia coast. The family legend is that Hudson Bay traders told William that the river was named to honour Joe Nahanee. The river had its own stories and legends. A tribe of native people had lived nearby, known as the Naha people. Over time, this tribe of people vanished without a trace. The name of the river and tribe added to a possible connection.

Maude Nahanee Thomas 1901-1957.

The following is a biography of Maude Thomas, who passed away in August of 1957. Maude was one of Cecilia's children with William. This story appeared in an article for the newspaper the Brotherhood of BC.:

* Maude's story is told as she is talking and therefore moves back and forth in time, and she would change the period she is referring to in an account of her life. *

"I was born in 1901 in Moodyville. That was the name of a mill located below 3rd Street hill in North Vancouver. But, of course, it wasn't 3rd street then. My father worked for the mill. Dad had his second-class engineer's papers and ran a donkey engine.

My mother named me Maude, the same name as the first schoolteacher, Maude Browse. She taught at the first White school in Moodyville, and she asked my mother to name me after her, so my mother did. I started to go to school in Moodyville when I was seven. We moved to the Mission reservation, where my mother had lived.

My mother was a member of the Skwxwú7mesh tribe. She got so lonesome for her sisters that she wanted to return to the reservation. Mom and dad needed permission to live at the Mission reservation. My dad got permission from the old chief. The chief agreed in return for finishing work on the church. The church is still standing today, down 3rd street in North Vancouver. My father built those two spires. It took him a long time, nearly two years. He sold two lots he had in North Vancouver to buy the materials to finish the work on the church.

My two brothers and I registered in St. Paul's Residential School. We were signed in until we were sixteen. It was almost compulsory for every Indian child on the Indian Reserve to be registered at the school and stay until sixteen. We lived at the school, even though our home was on reserve. The girls and boys were allowed home on alternate Saturdays, just for the day, and we had some days at Christmas and Easter, plus two months in the summer. I think schooling was made compulsory by the Indian Department to force us to get an education. Of course, there was religious pressure from the church, too. They wanted us to get our training in religion. My oldest brother just went into school to study our faith because he was sixteen when he moved there.

They were very strict at school, but we got good schooling. They taught us to knit and embroider. The boys learned woodworking and things like that. No one at any time could speak the Indian language, not even a word. I blame that for today. Now hardly anyone can talk about the language only if your parents voice it all day long is there a chance to learn. I can understand some words, but it is hard to speak.

Sometimes the sisters would tell us that we were " Dirty Indians" and that they had made a great sacrifice in coming out from France to teach us. They gave us a terrible inferiority complex, and some of us never really get over feeling how inferior the white people think we are. There was one very kind sister. Her name was Reverend Mother Aimee. Sometimes she would sit for a whole hour to make some point. The sisters are so busy, and there are so many children in the classroom that they can't spend time like that.

When I was 14, the Indian Agent from Indian Affairs went to my father and told him that I had passed grade eight, as far as the school went. My brother was fifteen, and it was the same with him. The agent wanted my father to send me to the East to get more education because there wasn't any way to go on here. My mother was very sick then and didn't want me to go because I was the eldest girl. The doctors said that my mother had Tuberculosis, consumption they called it. They said that she would linger for a long time, so I stayed on at the school. The nuns would not let me leave school even though I had finished my schoolwork. I read those books backward and forwards. There wasn't anything else to read. The school let me go home for about three hours twice a week, and I did the washing and some of the housework.

My mother could have gone to Tranquille, but she didn't want to go so far from home. She had her bedding and her dishes. So, we kept everything separate and sent her bedding to the laundry. When I'd leave her, I'd always want to kiss her, but she wouldn't let me-" Just on the forehead," she'd say.

My mother was a very devout woman. I would read all the stories of the saints to her. That taught me something. I noticed that poor people always have miracles happen to them. I thought how wonderful some of the stories were.

At first, I thought I would like better education, but I wanted to be with my mother. I saw from my father that education was important. He had his papers for a steam engineer, and he could have gone a long way if he had had an education."

[Maude loved her father and loved to spend time with him. She learned of his interests in Indian land claims. People like Andy Paul and Joe Capilano discussed land claims with their fellow workers. They became involved in the political struggle and became famous across Canada. Reverent Peter Kelly, another person who would raise his profile, originally from Skidekate. He was working with Indian people from all parts of British Columbia.

"William Nahanee worked with the Reverend Peter Kelly and helped form the Indian Rights Association in 1913. Rev. Peter Kelly used to write to us, and because my father had no schooling, I dictated his answers. So, when I wrote my father's letters, I was very interested in Indian affairs. I learned a lot from Rev. Kelly.

I came to live on the Burrard Reserve, about a mile east of the Second Narrows Bridge. There was no bridge then. I lived there with my husband in the house down by the creek. We had six children, but we lost one of them. My husband got a chance to go longshoring for Empire Stevedoring. My oldest brother was a boss there. So, we moved back to Mission Reserve, and while we were there, my husband got hurt on the job, and a month later, he died of spinal meningitis. When my husband died, my father-in-law said," Don't ever take your children off the reserve, don't ever marry outside. If you get a stepfather for the children, he'll never look after them. But if you marry someone from the reserve, he'll be both stepfather and uncle to your children, and he'll take good care of them.

When I was sixteen, I left school. My mother was sick, so the Victorian Order of Nurses nurse visited her daily. Then the boyfriend I had asked me to marry him. My boyfriend's parents went to my parents. That was the way marriage was arranged. My mother and father did talk about it for a long time. My mother knew that she didn't have long to live, and she wanted to see me married and in a home of my own. So she encouraged me to marry the boy, but she didn't say I had to marry him. We got married, and she'd give us something else and put it down differently in her books.

Even in 1950, my husband's father, grandpa, we called him, was only getting an $8.00 old Age Pension. Now the Old Age Pensioners get $22.00. The Native Brotherhood did that. In the past five years, the relief has been a little better. The mothers get $15.00. I should know; we were on subsidy for five months this year when my husband had his defective leg-$15.00 for Stan, my boy still at home, and $22.00 for the three of us, just because we lived on the reserve. I don't know how we can expect to live on that, even if we don't have to pay rent. There's still heat and phone and cooking expenses plus our food. Stan goes to high school, and h and ve shoes, clothes, and books. I'm telling you, my $15.00 paid for the oil, my boy's $15.00 paid for the power and phone, and we tried to live on my husband's $22.00.

I was only getting $5.00 relief for myself and four children. I don't know how I made it. I don't know what we'd have done if it wasn't for my brothers and sisters. I know the children were ragged sometimes. The government paid me $5. The government would only pay for specifics. The girl at the store was very kind, she knew my children had no father, and she'd sometimes give them a bag of oranges or a little bit of candy. I'd say to her, " I don't want lard-I can't use lard anymore. I've got nothing to fry in it."

My brother was visiting some of the reserves up in the interior recently. He said he saw one family with fifty pounds of lard stashed away under the bed- that was what the people received as part of their relief. The family had no way of using it up. I'd say, "I don't want any more beans-we can't eat beans that much."

Two years after my husband died, I married his younger brother. I had six children with him, and we lost three of them.

There was no road through the reserve when I married my second husband. We used to walk up through the reservation to Keith Road. A large mill at Dollarton had a little community there. There were two large boarding houses. One was run by a Hindu and the other by a Chinese. My second husband worked there till it closed. My mother-in-law and I used to go by canoe to Dollarton to sell our raspberries and cherries. I was always afraid of the current at Roche Point- that's Gates Park. One thing's for sure about the Indians we must help ourselves. If you don't speak up, no one will do anything. I could almost hear my father when he used to answer. Reverend Peter Kelly's letters, how depressed he was over the whole condition of the Indians, how oppressed they were, how pushed aside, how ignored. That's why I think my dad and Reverend Peter Kelly got together and ended up with the Native Brotherhood from right down to that.

I am a Counsellor for the Burrard band for the second time. The first time I served for two years, from 1935 to 1955, then in 1955, I was elected by acclamation. When I got sick, my eldest son, Leslie, took it for two years, but he found it was too much work. Then I was elected Counsellor again this year, and now I'm the secretary-Treasurer. I listen to the complaints and phone the Department for older people. If someone is hard up, I let the Department know and find out where the relief cheque is.

According to the Indian Agent, there won't be any Indian Reserves in ten years, not even in ten years. I can't see that. I don't think anyone wants to franchise, and I don't think anyone wants to sell outright. You can franchise off the reserve-that means you get your percent of the capital of our Indian Band fund. Two of my daughters married white men. They went around with Indian boys, but none had a steady job. When they married the white boys, they automatically left the Burrard Band, franchising out. But except for the odd one, the Indians don't want to leave the reserve. All they want is a fair stake. "

Mary See-em-ia 1840 – 1910

Her father, Kwelanewx, a Skwxwú7mesh man from Capilano (Xemelch'stn) whose name was Xaatsa'lanexw/Haat'salenewx, lived at Katzie. His wife came from Nicoman, in the Fraser Valley. Kwelanewx had a daughter, Mary, who grew up on one of the Katzie reserves, set aside for Indian people from other nations.

Mary's grandmother cared for her. Mary told her family about how her grandmother raised her. Granny, as she called her, taught Mary many things. Granny taught her many traditional Salish arts and crafts, including Salish weaving and goat blanket weaving. Mary also learned about the skills needed for living on the land. Mary also learned about the traditional songs of her people. It became her duty to pass on the information. Mary had to keep these practices alive and inspire others to use traditional knowledge and experience to build their distinctive, successful, and creative lives.

Mary learned that the mountain-goat had been a member of the Pitt Lake tribe transformed by the Transformer's helpers, so it stands in a special relationship with the Katzie. Mountain goats were numerous on the mountains above the shores of Pitt Lake. As well as hunting goats for their wool, Katzie people ate goat meat. The wool from the goat was hung for a while, then prepared for use by the tribe or traded with other tribes for items such as canoes, paddles, and food not available in Katzie communities, such as dried clams and dried herring.

Mary was a winter Spiritual Dancer, following in her father's footsteps. She accompanied him to the other Salish communities that held winter dances. The Katzie people had weekly winter dances and potlatches between October and April in the mild winter months.

The family knew Mary was well known throughout the Fraser Valley and always spoke English. Mary and her father often went to Fort Langley to trade and shop for supplies. She met William Eihu, and they were soon married. Eihu, a pureblood Hawaiian man, had come from Hawaii and worked for the Hudson Bay Company. There is no record of his parents or the family he may have left behind, but he did bring a bible with him.

This Christian Bible in the Hawaiian language was one of the first bibles in Gastown. William Eihu arrived in Fort Langley from the Hawaiian Islands sometime in the mid-1840s.

Before William came to Fort Langley, he had been a teacher in native Hawaiian schools. He settled at Fort Langley and was one of their first employees. Mary and William Eihu fell in love and were married at the fort. When Eihu's contract ended, they moved to New Westminster for a few years. In New Westminster, Mary and William Eihu had a baby girl named Margaret. After Margaret was born, the family moved to Vancouver. In Vancouver, Eihu found work at the Hastings Mill. The mill owned a store, a housing complex, and a school. Joe Nahinu met William Eihu at the Mill and became good friends. They lived beside each other at the Mill. Mary became so attracted to Joe that they had a baby girl and named her Lucy.

While the men worked at the mill, Mary raised chickens, pigs, and a vegetable garden. She sold her farm products to the people who lived close to them.

People said that the Mill owner, Capitan Raymur, did not like to see these animals running all over the sawmill sawdust. So Raymur asked them to move. So, in 1869, Joe, William Eihu, Mary and their family moved to a small property on the edge of Stanley Park in Coal Harbour. Joe, William Eihu and Mary took out Canadian citizenship on August 4th, 1871, in Victoria, British Columbia.

Mary See-em-ia was a woman of great aptitude who raised three children and loved two men in the wilderness of Stanley Park. She made countless contributions to the growth of British Columbia. She taught her friends and neighbours goat's wool weaving and Salish dog wool weaving. These were skills she had learned while growing up at Katzie. She also taught about harvesting seafood, growing fruits and vegetables and holding feasts. Mostly, Mary loved gardening; it was her passion all her life that she passed this passion to her descendants. One of her legacies was that she planted many cherry trees near the entrance to Stanley Park [many of these trees still exist].

 Mary stood up for her rights and taught her family members through example. She had learned English as a young girl and taught her family the importance of English, the colonizers' language. This skill helped her when she went to court to fight for her rights. As a result, many of her descendants would become great leaders who would also stand up for the rights of the Indian people. We will learn this as we read about her many descendants who fought for the rights of the Indian people. Unfortunately, Mary passed away in 1905.

During her life at the Kanaka ranch, Joe Nahinu and William Eihu chose a site where they cleared enough land to build two cabins on a tiny clearing made on the shore with a creek running through it. Thus, they had natural water for their garden and animals. While Joe and Eihu worked at the mill or made charcoal and sold it to the Hastings Mill, See-em-ia started another garden. She also raised chickens and pigs. As neighbours, Joe and William visited back and forth. Other Hawaiians lived in the area, so the area became known as the Kanaka Ranch. It became quite a large area, with cabins at the Rancheria property and other cabins built in the forest that led into Stanley Park, as it later became known. These mixed-blood people that settled there were mainly Hawaiians who had intermarried with Indian wives.

The women were a mixture of Skwxwú7mesh, Whu-Muthqueam, and Tsleil-Waututh people, and they developed friendships and worked together as their husbands worked together in the industries around Burrard Inlet. The women, skilled in weaving, spent much time weaving goat's wool and cedar bark. They would have made many blankets with goat's wool, Salish Wooly Dog hair and cedar bark material. They travelled by canoe to trade with the Katzie and Skwxwú7mesh people, exchanging store-bought foods for the raw wool and cedar bark.

The men had learned other forms of making money, such as making charcoal. The extra money allowed people to attend winter activities. With guidance from Joe and Eihu, the men had learned to make charcoal and sell it to the mills. The children of these families, who called the Rancheria their home, trekked daily to school at the mill. As the number of families grew, the trails became broad and well-used. Over time, many families moved away. Some went to North Vancouver, Usthahn and Moodyville. Other families blended into the growing city of Vancouver. During the Nahanee family's life at the Kanaka Ranch, Morten had pre-empted land in the area known as Coal Harbour. He did this without first determining that some families had already settled at Coal Harbour. Maybe Morton did know but went to court to have the people at the Kanaka Ranch evicted in any event. He lost the case as Mary Eihu had lived on the land since 1869. In 1899, the Supreme Court ruled in her favour and guaranteed her title to her land. However, a real estate dealer was so anxious to get the Kanaka Ranch land that he broke her fences and took five/sixths of her land. He also burned three dwelling houses. Mary then worked with a lawyer to appeal to the city of Vancouver. Her children, William Nahanee and Margaret McPhee nee Eihu, helped her get the money to pay a lawyer for the court case.

Margaret (Minnie) McCord October 1877- 1937

From 1931 to 1956, the archivist, for Vancouver, Major James Skitt Mathews, did a series of interviews with people that interested him. He did several interviews with the Eihu/Nahanee family. In one instance, in 1936, Major Mathews recorded his interview with Margaret McCord, the only child of Mary

See-em-ia and William Eihu. She told Major Mathews that she married Ben McCord, a gold rush miner. Ben came to Burrard Inlet and logged for Jerry Rogers at Jericho Beach. There he met Margaret. Major Mathews interviewed the family. In the interview, Margaret told Mathew they were married by Rev. Thos Derrick at the little church on Water Street. Mathews said that maybe it was called the Indian Church or Wesleyan Methodist Church. Be that as it may, it was the first church in Vancouver. In the interview, she stated that she was the only child of Margaret and Ben McCord. In October 1877, Minnie was baptized in the same church where her parents were married. Minnie grew up with her grandmother at the Kanaka ranch. She remembers that her grandmother always wore boots. Minnie was a pupil at the Hastings Saw Mill school in her youth. Her aunt Lucy and Uncle William had to walk along a trail from the ranch to the school and from Georgia Street to Dunlevy Avenue.

Mary taught Minnie many skills and was especially concerned that Minnie spoke and understood English. In each succeeding Nahanee generation, the children learned English more than Skwxwú7mesh, partly because the Catholic church and government banned the Skwxwú7mesh language. In the interview, Minnie related that her mother died in April 1925. Margaret's grave is in Mountain View Cemetery, Vancouver. Her father, Ben, left and went over the Skagway Trail in 1898. He died the following year and was accorded the first Masonic funeral in Dawson City.

Minnie was a young woman at the John Morton events and paid little attention to the land's going on. She would have little knowledge about concerns of the land and so did not know much about John Morton and what he did. Minnie only knew from listening to the family talk about what was going happening learned over time that, in 1895, her mother [Margaret] and uncle had to give a lawyer some money, and that was how she [Mary] got the land; but it was pre-emption. Mary could live on the property but was not allowed to sell it.

In October 1899, Mary Eihu wrote a letter to Mayor and the city council. She talked about how she and her husband squatted on a piece of land fronting Coal Harbor in 1869. The land had 400 feet of frontage on Georgia Street, running north to the waterfront. Mary won the right to stay on her property forever. However, the terms were that the land could not be sold or given to anyone else. Mary did not receive a deed to the property, only the right to live there. Mary went to live with her son, William. Margaret and Dan ran the store for a few years. Finally, she was able to sell the land for $23,000. So ended life at the Kanaka ranch. The following is about what happened after moving from the Kanaka ranch.

When Mary See-em-ia died, her family buried her in the Capilano cemetery, West Vancouver. Note: Mrs. R.D. Smith [formerly Minnie McCord], 914 Pender Street west, presented her grandfather's bible to Vancouver in 1937.] In 2014, the Vancouver City council approved two lanes named after Mary See-em-ia and [William] Eihu.

Hazel Florence Nahanee 1910-1956

Hazel is the child of William Nahanee and Cecilia Johnny. The family was living on the Mission Reserve in North Vancouver. They had just returned to Cecilia's ancestral home.

Hazel attended St. Paul's residential school, located on land that had belonged to the Skwxwú7mesh First Nation. Like her brothers and sisters, Hazel was in residential school until she was 16. At the age of 17, 1927, Hazel married Frank Matthew Thomas. They made their home on the Burrard Reserve, along the Dollarton Highway.

Frank and Hazel had nine children: Gary, Kathleen, Lorna, Charlie, Peter, Jacqueline, Bonnie, Madeline, and Lei-Loni. These children also attended St. Paul's residential school.

Her children fondly recall that Hazel loved all her children equally, and she gave them chores equally. Hazel's next love was gardening. She grew all the vegetables the family needed, such as potatoes, carrots, beets, and onions. In addition, the family property had many fruit trees, including apples, pears, plums, and cherries.

To last us through the winter, Hazel canned what she could. Her flower garden produced flowers for the church on Sundays. Her children learned to appreciate and love gardening from their mother.

The family would go camping at the Indian River during the summer. Hazel, an environmentalist before her time, taught her children to leave the area as they found it. To clean up and don't destroy and leave only their footprints behind. Hazel had such a love for the land and animals. This love was to such an extent that she would rescue raccoons from the outhouse.

Her children remember that their mother had a wonderful sense of humour and a beautiful laugh. She couldn't carry a note for singing, but she could whistle a delightful tune. Hazel was a fascinating character and a loving person.

To earn extra money (the family was a large one) during hard times, she would dig seafood, crabs, and clams to sell. Hazel took her to the beach to harvest seafood. Hazel also went into the woods to collect Barberry bark (cascara) from cutting up, dry, and bag in burlap sacks to sell. Hazel also worked in a cannery, along with other relatives. Other work she did include working for a local artist, cleaning houses, and being a companion to her mother-in-law. Hazel's children loved her. She was always the best mother, loving and teaching them about life, their culture, and their way of life. This knowledge has sustained them throughout their life.

Gertrude Guerin 1917-1998

Gertrude "Gertie" Guerin, also known as ("Old War Horse"), chief, politician, community advocate, the elder (born 1917 in North Vancouver on the mission Indian reserve no 1; died 1998. Guerin was a fierce protector of First Nations people and culture. She represented the Musqueam nation locally as an elected chief and on the national stage in Canadian jurisdiction over traditional Musqueam territory challenges.

In 1953–54, Gertrude Guerin and her husband moved their family to his ancestral community of Musqueam in Vancouver. There, Guerin became engaged in advocacy work for First Nations people. She went on to be elected chief of the Musqueam. Gertie fought discrimination. Gertie learned to be passionate about her concerns. She learned to do this as a child, listening to people who visited her father. William's visitors included people involved in Indian policy. The visitors were concerned about Indian rights and titles.

Gertie grew up in North Vancouver on the Skwxwú7mesh Mission Reserve Number 1. Gertie's mother, Mary Jane, a Skwxwú7mesh Band Member, was the second wife of William Nahanee 1. Like her sister, Maude, Gertie would hang around with her dad as he visited the men who came to talk and discuss Indian politics. These people were Andrew Paull, Chief Joe Capilano, and Peter Kelly. These three men, who fought for native rights and issues, were part of the great leaders of native people in their day.

Gertie met Victor Guerin when he moved from Musqueam to live on the Mission reserve. Gertie, a strong woman, married Victor and lived at Sla7an. Victor worked on the waterfront as a longshoreman. They had four children: Delbert, Beverly, Glen, and Beryl. In 1953, they moved their family to Musqueam. In later years, Gertie became chief of the Musqueam People and accomplished many things for her people. She had a loud voice, self-determination, and strength of character during her public life.

In 1963, she became a founding member of the Vancouver Indian Center. She was the Executive Director and board member. The Friendship Centre, a charitable agency, provides health, welfare, social services, human rights, culture, recreation, and equality for all genders of aboriginal people of all ages. The Friendship Centre emphasizes the philosophies and values of varied aboriginal cultures and traditions. The VAFCS has also helped aboriginal people access education, housing needs, and support for families. The Friendship Centre strives to provide holistic and cultural services to all its community members.

In 1967, Ray Collins from the Department of Indian Affairs worked with Gertie to develop the Native Education Center. The center supports educational opportunities for Indian people in Vancouver. In 1979, the NEC transitioned to a private college and is now operated and controlled by the British Columbia Assembly of First Nations. The Native Educational Center continues to recognize the contributions of Gertrude Guerin with a Visionary Award in her name, an award given to leaders who have impacted the Indigenous community.

Gertrude Guerin advocated for social justice initiatives, where she sought to improve relations between law enforcement and members of Indigenous communities, who faced systemic racism and stereotyping. Guerin was a founding member of the Vancouver Police and Native Liaison Society.

Her son and other members of the Musqueam nation 1975 went to court against Indian Affairs for misrepresenting them and their interests. This case stemmed from actions taken by Indian Affairs in 1958, representing the Musqueam and leased approximately 162 acres of prime Vancouver land to the Shaughnessy Heights Golf Club. The Musqueam band won the case. The court awarded the band $10 million for the government's failure to provide all details of the agreement to the Musqueam. R v. Guerin is considered a landmark case in Canadian law, and fiduciary duty became central to Section 35 of the Constitution Act, 1982, which enshrines protections for Indigenous rights.

Origin & History – Salish Woolly Dogs and Other Women's teachings

The Salish Wool Dog originated in the Coast Salish (now known as Washington State and British Columbia) in the 18th century. Though they were decent at hunting, they were primarily bred for their fluffy fur and coat. They were strictly limited to gated caves and islands, so their white colour and the breed remained true. At a time, the Indigenous women of the Pacific Northwest's coastal regions paddled their canoes to small, rocky islands once a day or so to care for packs of small, white-furred dogs.

The dogs would greet them, yelping and pawing as they implored their keepers for food. The women, in turn, would pet the dogs and dispense a stew of fish and marine mammal bits—not scraps, but quality food. Once the dogs (most of them perhaps females, probably in heat) had eaten their fill, the women might linger a while to sing to them and brush their long white fur. The dogs—and their fur—were the women's source of wealth, and the women kept watch to ensure that no village cur crept onto the islands to taint the breed.

Once or twice a year, the women arrived as usual with a supply of food but also brought mussel-shell knives. The dogs knew the routine: settle down and relax so the women could cut away their white tresses, shearing the dogs as closely as shearers do sheep.

Back in their village longhouses, the women transformed that fur into yarn, spinning it and mixing it with the wool of mountain goats and adding plant fibres and goose down to make the thread solid and warm. They beat the yarn with white diatomaceous earth to deter insects and mildew. They dyed some of the yarn red with alder bark, tinted it a light yellow with lichen, and produced blue and black threads using minerals or huckleberries. The rest—an ivory-hued yarn—they set aside. Then the women set up their looms and weave, turning out twill-patterned blankets of various sizes, some with elaborate and colourful geometric designs, others with simple stripes. The dogs did more than provide fur. They were also part of village life: sometimes, a favourite woolly dog would keep a weaver company.

The finely woven blankets symbolized wealth and a connection to ancestors and the spirit world. They represented a person's generosity, too—significant numbers of blankets were given away at potlatches, gift-giving ceremonial feasts. The blankets had other uses as well. Sometimes they wrapped together a couple in a marriage ceremony or adorned a chief, while smaller ones might swaddle a newborn or were worn as garments. People used blankets to negotiate the purchase of brides and enslaved people or settle disputes. Blankets cloaked chiefs and other members of the nobility for burial. Proud owners stored their blankets in scented cedar boxes.

Indigenous oral traditions attest to a robust weaving industry in some coastal nations—such as the Cowichan on British Columbia's Vancouver Island and the Skwxwú7mesh on British Columbia's southern coast—endured for thousands of years.

Eighteenth-century European explorers wrote about seeing flocks of wool dogs and observing people robed in blankets partly woven from the canines' fur. (Morell, 2021) They sewed and patched clothing, traded with their neighbours for outgrown items, and made do with colder homes. The women were unpaid workers. They continued to do as always, cook, clean, budget, shop, and care for the children. Many women also worked outside the home or took boarders, did laundry for trade or cash, and did sewing for neighbours in exchange for something they could offer. The Skwxwú7mesh people had always helped extended families. Auntie Maude and her sisters were grateful they had nephews and cousins who came to fix plumbing and other house repair work. Some worked at fish canneries and fruit canneries. (Wyss B. 2020)

Or many worked as domestics and in restaurants. However, these jobs disappeared as unemployment spread in greater Vancouver. Women factory workers typically handled clothing and food. Very few Skwxwú7mesh women had more than grade five education. Companies were hiring only men. Therefore, factories hired men first. Men took jobs as clerical workers, teachers, nurses, telephone operators and even domestics. Men were willing to take lower-paying jobs just to be employed.

In 1936, another amendment was directed to all Indian Agents to allow Indian agents to control band council meetings and cast a deciding vote in case of a tie. The Indian Act determined what Indian bands could be allowed to do. This would continue until 1985 when the legislation would discuss Indigenous nations' self-governance.

1899   St. Paul's Indian Residential School

The first church was erected in 1863 at Sla7an, and the current church was finally built-in 1884. By 1899 Bishop Durieux instructed the Skwxwú7mesh people to build St. Paul's Indian residential school. He followed the design of other Indian residential schools built across BC and other provinces. The purpose of the school was to separate the children from their parents and grandparents. This separation increased the assimilation of the children. At the school, the children became bilingual.

Eventually, however, the students would learn to be English-speaking only. The elderly Skwxwú7mesh knew only Skwxwú7mesh. The parents spoke broken English. The children in the school learned only English, math, European history, religion, and the colonial way of life. They did not understand the Skwxwú7mesh language, culture, or creation stories. If the children ran away, the RCMP found them and returned them to the school. The school would be open until it was torn down in 1959.

Daily life in residential school....

The children were kept at the school until they were 16. Then, the nuns sent the students home, whatever their grade was. As a result, some children received only a grade of four or five level. In time, this was not high enough to secure suitable employment.

At the school, there were to be no visits from their families. This way enforced the assimilation policy. When the children could go home, they could not talk to their grandparents because they did not know English. Likewise, the parents could not speak to the children because they knew only broken English.

So, before the school opened, the bishop arranged for the sisters of the Child Jesus to provide the education. On October 5, 1898, the sisters arrived from Le Puy, France. The bishop was familiar with the organization and decided that he wanted them to operate the school. The first three nuns were Sister Felicien, Sister Joannes and Sister Hieronymie. Sister Felicien could speak English and soon began to teach it to the other two while they waited for the school to open.

At St. Paul's Indian residential school in North Vancouver, Indian Affairs registered 43 girls at the residential school and 57 boys. The children were in grade one to grade eight. The girls' names were Emma Isaac, Mary Magdalene George, and Josephine Lacket-Joe. Many Skwxwú7mesh people provided services for St. Paul's church: Mary Ann [Dan Paul's wife]; August Billy and Grandpa Nahanee worked on the spires and windows; Christine Jack and Cecilia Nahanee helped prepare the dead and helped look after the sick, and Old Daniel was the first bellringer.

The Skwxwú7mesh Nation was one of the bands with a residential school on its reserve. The students were from Skwxwú7mesh, Musqueam, Mount Curry and Sechelt. The students were in different age groups, starting at three years. Indian Affairs kept good records of children admitted to the school.

Here is an example of a partial list of the girls that were in from 1918 to 1929

#	name	admitted age	left date	grade
85	Madeline	1918, 7	9/1826	8
86	Carmelita	10/18	9/1929	8
87	Florence	10/1918, 7	9/1929	8
88	Hilda	10/1918	9/1928	10
89	Carrie	10//1918,5.5	9/1921	3
90	Eva	10/1920,6.5	9/1927	7
91	Sarah	10/1920, 8	9/1925	2
92	Bernadette	10/1920, 10	9/1922	2
93	Violet	10/1920, 10	9/1922	2
94	Lena	1920,9	9/1922 (Jacobs Monica, Skwxwú7mesh Nation)	

Our people built the Church that the priests asked for with their money. This began the entrenchment of the church and the residential school, fully bringing the Skwxwú7mesh children to be indoctrinated to be assimilated into the English settler society. (Wyss B. 2020)

Stories of daily life in residential school...
St. Paul's Indian residential school opened on January 23, 1899. Cornelia Carrasco was the first girl. She was eight years old. Her father was from Chile, and her mother was a METIS. She grew up in an English-speaking family. The school was happy to accept her. Cornelia would be an asset to the school because she could help other students to learn English. Ellen, Rosy, Amelia Gonzales, and Rita were the next three girls. Also enrolled were children whose names were Amy and Sheila. Their father died at the sawmill where he worked. Their mother could not care for them, so she brought them to the residential school. The girls were five and six years old. When the principal learned the story, she accepted the children. The girls were assigned a number, which became their name until they left the school. Amy and Sheila started school in

grade one. They cried every night because they missed their mother. The girls returned home when they were 16 and 17.

Their day started at 6 am. The nun woke everyone up, and the girls kneeled by their beds for the morning prayer. Then they got dressed, lined up and went down to the chapel for the morning mass. After mass, the girls went to the main activity room. In the room, the girls lined up again. When it was their turn, Sheila said her number and opened her mouth. The nun squired some cod liver oil in her mouth. Then Sheila was asked to repeat her number. Thus, the nun would know that Sheila had swallowed the cod liver oil. Then the girls were lined up to go to the dining room.

The breakfast meal was porridge served on a metal plate and toast. After breakfast, the girls could play outside the yard if the weather was good.

At 9:00, the school bell rang. All the children ran to their classrooms. It was time to learn their alphabet, arithmetic, reading, and writing. At St. Paul's School, the added subject was religion. The school had only one book for students to learn to read. The book was called Dick and Jane. They had to read the book until they knew every word and read it aloud. After reading, the students studied arithmetic.

After school, the children could play in the yard. While they were out there, the nun brought them sandwiches. The sandwiches were slices of bread and margarine. On Fridays, they had peanut butter sandwiches. At 5:00 pm, the children went to the activity room. The girls would learn to mend socks and fold clothes. While they did this, the supervisor would help them recite the prayer, called the rosary. It is a long prayer. Then, at 6:00, the children lined up for supper. Sheila and Amy were good boarding pupils who were always obedient. But sometimes, Amy wanted to play and not pray. Sheila and Amy lived this way for the next seven years.

Most of a student's day involved cooking and cleaning the school building. In addition, the school was so underfunded that proper care, such as repairs, was left undone. Another fact, the school was becoming overcrowded; students were underfed, malnourished, deprived of medical care, and improperly clothed during the winter months. The Skwxwú7mesh community came forward to help with the food costs in the first year.

However, when Indian Affairs took over funding the school, the Skwxwú7mesh people stopped bringing food. To help with costs, the nuns sewed uniforms for the students.

Sometimes, in later years, the merry-go-round would be their fondest memories of the school; some memories were not so fond. The children would experience severe abuse at the school from the nuns, priests, and older students. The principal was cruel and the punishment unreasonable. Students had to kneel in the main hall for hours. The nuns would also strap the students. The nuns would speak in French, so children would not know what the nuns were saying. (B. Wyss) Some children ran away from the school. However, the school called the RCMP to find the children and return them.

As a result, many children suffer health problems. In addition, both girls and boys experienced rape by the priests and other staff running the schools and older schoolmates. Indian Affairs, the RCMP and the Roman Catholic church, together, worked towards the genocide of the Skwxwú7mesh people. Among the things done were, changing people's names to Anglican words. A number was given to each student, which meant that if inquiries were made about anyone, only the student number could identify anyone, making it difficult to find anyone. The parents were not allowed to visit their children. The children who were brothers and sisters at the school were not allowed to mingle with each other. (Wyss B. 2020)

At St. Paul's Residential School, the girls and boys were members of different activities. The girls were in dance groups. Some nuns made the costumes needed for the dance routines. The boys were in boxing, taught by Alex Strain. The nuns also made the boys' shorts to prepare for boxing tournaments.

In July 1900, Indian Affairs announced funding the school at $5.00 per student. As a result, the school received $150 for 30 students. However, the money was insufficient to feed the students, buy school supplies, janitorial supplies or clothe them.

In 1920, Duncan Campbell Scott, deputy director of Indian Affairs, worked with leaders of the religious groups most involved in native education. He then revised the Indian Act.

The Act forced Indian people to send their children to a residential school from ages seven to fifteen to attend either an Indian residential school or a day school. (Facing History and ourselves)

Scott favoured residential schools for Indian children as he believed removing them from the influences of home would hasten the cultural and economic transformation of the whole Indian population, thus eliminating "the Indian problem."

When he mandated school attendance in 1920, he stated, "I want to eliminate the Indian problem. I do not think the country should protect a class of people who can stand alone continuously. Our objective is to continue until no Indian in Canada is protected by the Indian Act. and there is no Indian question, and no Indian Department, that is the whole object of this Bill. (Facing History and ourselves)

St. Paul's Indian residential school had both day scholars and residential students.

My father and his siblings had to attend as residential students. They were of school-age when Scott created his changes to the Indian Act. 50% of the students enrolled in St. Paul's residential school were children of Nahanees in the early 1900s. (Wyss B. 2020)

Communication was allowed in only English, which many Skwxwú7mesh children did not understand when they first arrived at the school in the first years of its operation. Religion was to be practiced every day by attending mass every morning, learning prayers during the day in class, and more praying from 5: 00 to 6:00 pm.

The students would learn to be English-speaking only. The elderly Skwxwú7mesh knew only Skwxwú7mesh. The parents spoke broken English. The children in the school learned only English, math, European history, religion, and the colonial way of life. They did not understand the Skwxwú7mesh language, culture, or creation stories. If the children ran away, the RCMP found them and returned them to the school. The children had to write letters home in English, which meant their parents would not understand the writing. The priests and nuns who ran the school withheld any gifts or letters their parents sent back. (Wyss. 2020)

The children were kept at the school until they were sixteen. Then, the nuns sent the students home, whatever their grade was. As a result, some children only reached grade four or grade five. In time, this was not high enough to secure suitable employment.

When the children could go home, they could not talk to their grandparents because they did not know English. Likewise, the parents could not speak to the children because they only knew broken English. They did get medical care; however, the nuns often kept the students at the school for three or four days before sending them to the hospital. For example, my father was held at the school for three days when he became ill. The nun said that it was God's will. My father had his ankle crippled, which meant he would be on crutches for the rest of his life. (Wyss.2020)

Children only spent a few hours in the classroom and many hours working on chores assigned by the nuns during school hours. By the time they left the school, they had attained a grade level of five. The result was that they were able only to get low-level employment. When they left school at 16, the students could go home. They lost their grandparents, who had passed away. The children were a lost people. They couldn't speak Skwxwú7mesh and could only identify with the colonialist. The students did not receive love at the school. Their parents didn't love them because they didn't know these young people who came home. The children became survivors of a horrible life of sexual, mental, emotional, and physical abuse. Some then became abusers themselves because that was what they learned. The depression of the everlasting feeling of isolation, as well as the fact that the children were raised without love or care in these schools, resulted in a vicious cycle of physical, emotional, and sexual abuse survivors, who were (and still are,) unable to love and care for their children (B. Wyss, survivor).

When children entered residential school, they knew only Skwxwú7mesh and its way of life. Removing the children to residential schools caused the students to become bilingual. The bilingual language did not last long. Students learned a new culture, that of the dominant society, English. The parents were not allowed to visit their families at the residential school. The school lessons were only about math, reading and writing in English. They also learned religion. Only the colonial way of life was meaningful for the teachers to implement in the children's minds.

When the children went home, they did not know anything about the history of the Skwxwú7mesh people or their traditions, way of life or roles of their elders. The children met at school and did not know who they were. In the old way of life, the parents would decide the children's future mates. At the school, children met strangers and were attracted to people they might never have gotten to know. As a result, the children chose mates the parents did not know.

The teachers flourished in degrading the children in their charge. The teachers told the students that they were dumb, ignorant, and wrong about Indian people. Sandra believed her teachers. The teachers were adults, so they must know right or wrong. Teachers must know the truth about what they are saying. If the teacher told her the Indian language, customs, and ideas were awful, the teacher must be right.

Teachers used the strap or forced Sandra to kneel for hours in a public place where other students would see her enforce their teachings. Sandra was at the residential school for four years. When she left school, Sandra believed that it was a bad thing to be an Indian. However, Sandra began to go to counselling sessions and workshops. It would take decades for Sandra to believe in herself finally. Sandra started telling her children they had self-worth, encouraging them to believe in themselves. To follow the history and true path of her people. (History sharing, 2020)

1900 Skwxwú7mesh people

The Skwxwú7mesh people have had many things written about them. Very little written and recorded is in the indigenous worldview that existed before contact. Sharing of this knowledge will be expanded using the existing research and written knowledge created after 1900 by other than Skwxwú7mesh people. I offer a statement from Verma Behari 1956, "Before the Skwxwu7mesh amalgamation, the community or village site was called "uxwimixw." The leader was a male chief with a nobility that included male and female leaders. (Verma, 1956) Verma does a good job researching and investigating the Skwxwú7mesh people. Before writing his thesis, he stayed with Skwxwú7mesh Families and spent years researching and collecting political, cultural, and social structures. The history is accurate enough. The writing's flaws come from a colonial settler's language and prose.

They often miss the deeper, much bigger meaning of kinship relationships and social and "political" structure with the Skwxwú7mesh. The label of nobility is inaccurate; the closer descriptive relationship would be language such as "siyam" – respected, elder, or head of the family. Verma relied heavily on the research of Anthropologist Charles Hill-Tout (a Eurocentric Anthropologist) to determine a version of History and create a story of Society and governing structure to what Skwxwú7mesh life was like before the change to Colonial governing structure imposed by incoming British rule. His argument is flawed in the structure by the lack of an indigenous worldview and methodology of writing. Daniel Heath Justice provides a valid explanation of this idealism of colonial settler opinions; the underlying use of language creates a misunderstanding of how Skwxwú7mesh History has evolved and been presented by many writers and researchers of Indigenous history. The need to decolonize the history for Skwxwú7mesh families to share their collective stories in a different light. (Heath Justice, Culture and Society)

Charles Hill Tout's descriptions of what he viewed as primordial Skwxwú7mesh political power culture, the essential "uxwimixw" of the early contact period were in the Skwxwú7mesh Valley:

The people lived in small, orderly villages. They consisted primarily of extended families. They had a headman who cared for the people and kept a tidy, governed community. The criteria for choosing a headman included birth order, material and non-material property ownership, liberal sharing of content property with others, industry, humility, and occupational efficiency. The qualities, such as generosity, good manners, honesty, industry, wisdom, and skill, which the Skwxwú7mesh demanded from the house group's head, were practiced. The children were obliged to get up early in the morning. After getting up, they bathe in the cold river water and rub their bodies with cedar boughs to clean them. The children learned habits of industry and cleanliness from a young age—the children's etiquette and behaviour befitting a respected man or woman by example and word of mouth. (P. 35 – 65.) (Verma, 1956) The references above only cover the surface of meaning in many processes. Such as the importance of their ancestral names. They learned that a name lived forever and that they should not do anything to bring shame to it. The value of correct behaviour, habits of industry, and active seeking of respect from others by liberal distribution of property were repeatedly impressed. This emphasis on seeking care from others was a powerful instrument of social control.

Your name in the ceremony meant this was how you were known in the spiritual world. Colonial names given did not have the same depth of meaning. Today we call these names our colonial or nicknames to refer to how we are labelled and followed by the government in our lifetime.

Education, Work, and the Church – the community around residential schools
Pre-contact through the transition to settler interruption...

Education of the child by the grandparent was a stabilizing tradition. Grandparents taught language, customs, stories of ancestors and spiritual origin stories. The time spent with grandparents left parents to hunt, forage, and harvest needed food, medicines, clothing and building shelter materials. The opportunity to gather for trade with other people farther north was essential to a diverse food supply.

In the past, the Skwxwú7mesh Families, each with a headman, lived in large family longhouses that could hold several generations within. These longhouses were built out of Cedar and could be up to 60' wide and 90' long. These longhouses would be more significant for housing up to hundreds for a gathering. These longhouses were in the center of the community. The main longhouse on Xwáy̓xway (Lumberman's Arch) was about 200' long and over 60' wide. This was removed around 1870 – when Lord Stanley and the City of Vancouver dedicated the park to Lord Stanley. (Matthews, 1955)

With industrialization and commerce, the Skwxwú7mesh people worked various jobs. They could engage in multiple games of chance, dance, sing, play drums and rattles, play ball games, and fish during their free time. Skwxwú7mesh people had a social system that provided sanctions for economic and ritual activities. Therefore, the combined economic, social and marriage alliances with other nations and communities across turtle island. Family stories of people who went east to marry as far as Manitoba during the fur trade.

The Community begins to Change to Colonial Settler ways of being...

A significant change from the Village of Sla7an to the Mission Reserve was the catholic church, which operated in the village from 1880 onwards. With the establishment of many businesses, the Skwxwú7mesh people experienced full cash employment. Usthahn became a larger community, with the church at its center. Some were new families, like Andrew Paul's and Chief Joe Capilano, who moved to the Mission so that the men could work in the new industries developing around Burrard Inlet. Some families, like Andrew Natrall, Rivers, and Guerrero, branched out into their homes when children grew up and married. In the early years of the Mission reserve, all houses had gardens and fruit trees.

However, Indian Affairs, through Parliament, used the Indian Act used to impose many restrictions meant to be used as barriers to continuing traditionally based social progress. The Royal Commission of 1913-1916 McKenna-McBride created the policy that would forever change the direction of the Skwxwú7mesh Families. The imposition of the Pass system, Potlatch ban laws and residential schools would forever decide the fate of Skwxwú7mesh Children and their Familie,s who were forced from their home communities to put their children in the Residential Schools. This mass relocation meant the home communities would be left for more extended periods than pre-contact (not abandoned but forced relocation by Government interference. (Government of Canada. 1913-1916)

Indian Affairs changed its title of headman to Chief, then created councillors. Indian Affairs also decided how many would be the chief and council. This would make the Superintendent of Indian Affairs the Skwxwú7mesh Chief and Council Chair for decades to come. Indian Affairs determined its role and what it could do or not do. These regulations and laws are in the Indian Act, a Canadian act of Parliament concerning registered Indians, their bands, and the system of Indian reserves. The Act dictated all aspects of the Indian peoples' lives. A review of the Indian Act shows how many changes were made and when. The Indian people, for many years, were not consulted about any new changes. Finally, the Department of Indian Affairs began to impose stricter rules and only went to Parliament to create adaptations.

The colonial government of Indian Affairs would dictate the development of Membership codes, governing structure, and daily life. The implementation would impact matriarchs and knowledge keepers, traditional people of the Skwxwú7mesh. Provincial policy on Indigenous peoples and the Nations' development of its governing in later years was designed to eradicate the existence of Matrilineal lines.

The membership code, for example, was created and implemented with Indian Affairs and Northern Development before the Legislation in 1981. This happened before the actual return of enfranchised Skwxwú7mesh Women and created a continued inequality for women today within the Skwxwú7mesh Membership. This unaddressed constitutional issue for Skwxwú7mesh women and their children is the most significant inequality and ongoing constitutional issue. The membership codes for the nation have all been based on unequal treatment for the women of Skwxwú7mesh and continue to exist. They will eradicate the lineage of these women by denying membership to their children and grandchildren. This does not always impact the men still today. (Squamish Naton, 1987)

Church and its impact on Skwxwú7mesh people

The Church forced the Community of Skwxwú7mesh people to build the church at the cost of the people. The initial building was around $11,000 for the establishment of the church.

The church's influence on the community was present in daily life. The women helped keep the church clean and brought flowers from their gardens for the alter. The men served as altar boys in their youth, and a few remained as servers when they grew older. Louis Miranda remained as the bell ringer every Sunday until he could no longer make it to the church. The teachings of the colonial settlement were becoming the primary way of Skwxwú7mesh life. The insidious efforts of church and government were permeating the fabric of the Skwxwú7mesh families in their homes and work and leisure time spent in service to the church. The children raised in the residential school were fully operational by the 1930s. The way of Skwxwú7mesh life was changing to a lesser version of the colonial settlements it was surrounded by.

Church influenced changes in the community.

The community would hold events to raise money for minor repairs to the church, not for the practice of feasting, which redistributed wealth and goods among the people equally; the church wanted these practices stopped and worked with Government and RCMP to ensure this type of fundraising and feasting would bring those efforts only to the church and their needs to educate Skwxwú7mesh People in the colonial ways. The ongoing influence and coercion of the church to hold the community members in compliance with Church edicts meant

Skwxwú7mesh people would forever be compliant to the Catholic Church, for instance, the need to create efforts to support this church and its staff – Priests and Nuns.

The church was built in the Mission reserve at its center, a house for the Priest and the home for nuns and their school. The fund-raising events included baking goods, bringing items to sell at the event and raffles. Women like Eva, Jenny and Rose were well known for being excellent home-baked bread and pie makers. Their baked goods always went quickly. The people loved the raffles, so they helped provide items and bought tickets to win the prizes.

Jimmy Nahanee was an excellent public speaker; people loved his coordination of the raffles. Jimmy had a ready smile and could tell stories about anything. The community homes became where only the husband, wife, and children lived. The grandparents, in-laws, and siblings of the parents lived elsewhere. (Wyss.202)

Deconstruction of the Skwxwú7mesh Original Governing to Squamish

The other Skwxwú7mesh community developed in North Vancouver was the Capilano reserve no. 5. The reservation had only a few families living there at the time. Because they were a few miles from Sla7an, they could participate in some Skwxwú7mesh rituals, such as the longhouse winter dances. However, the Catholic church found a convert, Joe Capilano, to move to Capilano, to convert the people to Catholicism. The catholic priests had been anxious to transform the community members and force them to stop their ritual activities. For instance, the feasts and giveaways were contrary to colonial practices. Good Christians earned money to increase personal wealth. The Skwxwú7mesh people at Capilano raised cash and things to give away at special gatherings. The giant giveaway meant greater recognition that the family received. The missionaries successfully suppressed the ritual gatherings for several years. However, several families continued the rituals in private. The potlatch ban law was created in 1884 to legally prevent ceremonial practices and ritual dancing of all indigenous peoples across Canada. (Mitchell, The Allied Indian Tribes of British Columbia: A study in pressure group behaviour, 1973) pg. 20. This would impact generations of knowledge keepers, and ceremonies would go underground to protect them and keep the practices up as our people had for centuries.

The Skwxwú7mesh people did have spiritual and ceremonial practices before Christianity came here. The Skwxwú7mesh believed in spiritual beings. They believed in spirits, such as the Xaays, the Transformers, or the shapeshifters: The Xaays, our Spiritual beings who walked amongst our people. Skwxwú7mesh origin stories are often based on the Xaays, siblings who travel together. They transform things like stone versions of a person or other living creature.[Siwash Rock in Stanley Park is a well-known example of the Xaays and their power to transform a human into stone. They all appear to someone to tell them some news. The missionaries needed to work hard to make the people give up these beliefs. The success of the priests and Indian Affairs was removing the children from their parents and grandparents to implement colonial-settler ways forcefully was the vehicle used by the Government, the rule of law and the church to determine the path to assimilation that the church desired. The government needed to take land, rights, and resources from the Skwxwú7mesh people.

Impacts on Skwxwú7mesh Women by church doctrine and Government policy
During the fur trade era, 1800-1900s, Skwxwú7mesh women were the only women living in the Greater Vancouver area. The Men of the fur trade and gold rush would come through the territory in enormous numbers crossing the mountains and coming up from south of the Fraser River and working in the fur, forestry industry, and industrialist sector. They were single men who had left families behind. They were French, English, Chilean, Scottish, Spanish, Swiss and Hawaiian.

The church involved itself in the affairs of the people and the fur trade by bringing their worldview of church and family, marriage, children, and societal views to the women of Skwxwú7mesh Nation. These views of society and how women were to behave became part of the deconstruction of the Matrilineal system of the Skwxwú7mesh People before contact. The expectation of changing the people came through the missionaries sent by the church to build the churches in Indigenous Communities to convert and assimilate the indigenous people. The priests would use indoctrination and bible teachings to accuse the indigenous women of living in sin with the settler men who lived with these women. The men either left to return to home communities or married, and the indigenous woman became the nationality of her husband and lost her indigenous identity.

This process would become the enforced rule of law with the legislation of Indian Affairs. The method of the enfranchisement of Indigenous women would happen for nearly 143 years before it would change under the Indian Act in 1985.

"When the church instituted the Durieux system, the bishop punished women for their sins. The sins were having a dirty house or doing laundry on Sunday. The sins included teaching their children the Skwxwú7mesh language, songs, and culture. Once a week, a Watchman visited all the homes to inspect and record any infractions. Then on Sunday, the whole village was gathered to hear about what happened during the week. The women were publicly in front of all the people. The men were never found guilty of any infractions". (Wyss. 2020)

The Durieux System was initially implemented to support isolating and containing indigenous people from the more significant white settlements to control and change these communities to more assimilated European social and political structures. The system was subject to be run by Oblates in these communities. (Mitchell, The Allied Indian Tribes of British Columbia: A study in pressure group behaviour, 1973)

Another example of enfranchisement through Indian Affairs, through the Indian Act, said that Indian women would lose their status when they married someone who was not the son of a Status man back three generations. If the department could prove that an illegitimate child was not a status Indian man, Indian Affairs stripped the child of its rights as a Status Indian (B. Wyss.,2020). Suppose the Indian man gave up his rights as a status Indian. The whole family lost their right. She could never return to the reserve if the woman left her husband. She would face jail time. If her family tried to give her fish, the Fish Officers took the fish away; she could be put in jail, fined, or both; I know this from personal experience.

"Aboriginal women cannot access treaty benefits, practice inherent rights to live on their reserve or inherit property. When a woman lost her rights, she also lost the right to be interned back home with their ancestors. One of the women fighting for her rights was Mary Two Axe Early. She said white people could bury their pets on the reserve land. However, the band did not allow her to do the same right. The Indian Act of Canada restricted access to their native community for any purpose." (Wyss. 2020)

"Aboriginal women without legal status could not participate in ceremonies and rituals on their traditional land. However, Indian men married whites, and their wives became status Indians. They could keep their status and give status to their wife and family. If the non-Indian wife had female children, the female child could not pass on Indian rights to the child—however, the male children could. Section 12, paragraph 1(1) of the Act worked to disadvantage the position of the Aboriginal women. It was considered an attempt to demolish Aboriginal families and alienate Aboriginal women from their land. Infliction of gender discriminatory laws, the Canadian government marginalized and disadvantaged Aboriginal women." (Wyss. 2020)

Spiritual and cultural traditions

The people practiced the whole immersion experience for youth to transition to adulthood and the next level of maturity. These practices and teachings are shared through oral transmission. Land-based experiential exercises from elders to youth learned methods of seeking a guardian spirit taught by grandparents, aunties, and uncles. When the children became adolescents, the boys and girls were encouraged to pursue connection to nature through a shokhwum [cold water bathing], fasting, sweat lodges, and undergoing physical hardships—toughening the body, building the capacity to bear hardships. And to develop self-reliance was also emphasized. The boys went alone to the woods to seek guardian spirits. Guardian spirits were supposed to confer varying powers ranging from those providing success in hunting and fishing to "Spirit" of different potency, including the ability to see people's future events or visions. The connection to spirit for youth manifests through songs and teaching granted through dreams and signs provided in the questions youth go through. These practices are handed down from generation to generation. These practices experienced significant interruption from layered colonial trauma. Today these practices still experience hardship in renewal and training.

At the time of her first "menstruation" – moon time, a girl was secluded for eight days because, during this period, this is the most potent time for a live giver; having this first moon time and the connection to spirit, it meant her first moon time was the most powerful of her life-giving cycle. Women needed to help her understand, and men would not interfere with these rituals. It signalled the beginning of the adult she would become. Her mother, aunties and grandmothers looked after her during this period, teaching her to be a woman and life-giver.

She was encouraged to busy herself with wool twining or basket weaving to show her how to learn patience for her home. She learned to make a ceremonial feast involving the distribution of gifts during this time. The men would be able to attend and participate as a community and family in the dinner and share this young woman's beautiful energy. Women's healing in this time is considered the highest, and bringing the community together to celebrate is a blessing for all the community.

In the case of a boy, the family sensed when the boy reached puberty. A feast was given to mark his first hunt. Young men would fast and practice Shokhwum and sweats, brushing themselves off with cedar to prepare for their first hunt. The importance of the first hunt is proving how they are ready to become a man and support their family and community to be prepared to be a mate and protector of their home fires. This first hunt is sacred to our young men. The feast is given to honour this hunt, and the meat is shared with the community of this young man and the gifts he is bringing to his adulthood and maturity.

The property owned by women included names from female ancestors, knowledge of ritual, dance, songs, spirit power, midwifery, weaving, basket making, harvesting of medicines, and processing and preserving foods and treatments. Women could weave intricate and robust ropes from the bark and roots of cedar fibres. The time of year to harvest, process, and use that cedar to incorporate the most intricate baskets, waterproof or nets for fishing, rope for tying, securing lodges and bog houses. These skills are required for knowing the time of year to gather. The time needed to cure is pliable and peak for the correct rope or basket.

The weaving of Salish Wooly dogs was known on the trade routes. The women kept and raised the dogs, harvested wool from them annually and used it to create dense, weather-resistant weavings of clothing and coverings. They gathered diatomaceous shells, which were pounded to a white powder – this kept bugs from the weaving and preserved the wool. The weaving was intricate and told stories. They gave the history of where you came from and were often family designs. The language was woven into these weavings in stories.

Traditional oral knowledge passed from mother to daughter, father to son; the sons would marry into a family and follow their wife to her home. Lands were often considered the home fires, and women kept the hearth. Mothers gave their sons names given to them by their mother's ancestors. For example, Louie's mother gave him the head of the house name when an ancestor passed away. Louie was not the eldest in the family group. Still, if the eldest son failed to show aptitude, lacked industry, initiative, wisdom or was otherwise incapable of adequately representing his house group, that name would be given to a family member who showed initiative and action.

Another example is Louie's family moved from their ancestral home at Chewelp to the mission reserve. His mother had established her own home, and she was the head of the house. The household leaders did not require it to be only male – the heads of household were the most appropriate and carried the knowledge and ways of the family and provided the direction for the family. Often, they were women. Matriarchs held counsel with men and advised the heads of house on several matters about daily life and dealing with the work of laying loved ones to rest in the proper ways.

Death

When death occurred, family and other houses had roles to support the family. Caretakers made sure the body was not left alone, the family asked for someone to come and sit, then the family gave gifts as an honorarium. Before touching the body, people would rub medicines on their hands. After this, he rubbed some on the relative. Next, historically our caretaker of the dead rubbed the body with medicines before washing it. And they would wrap them in a new blanket. All the time, the body faced east. After the preliminary preparations, the body was removed and driven to the cemetery.

The ceremony for the dead begins on the day of burial or cremation with the singing home of the loved one. This is done with the first daylight with the body. The family gathers before dawn and sings in the four directions to sing home to their loved ones. The XwáýXwáý Mask Dancers help the relative go home, and the women singers support these dancers and the helpers in performing these rites. Then the family goes to the river for Shohkwum to sing their power and strength for the day. Once this is done, they will sit and eat together and meet extended family for the ceremony and physical journey to the final resting place. The last day is spent performing the Burning Ceremony, where tables of kindling are prepared, and food for our relatives is made on a burning day.

The ceremony involves singing, prayers and celebration with family to help our relatives have all they need on the other side to go home to our family. We send clothes, blankets, food, tools, and personal belongings. These items are given up in the smoke to transition to the other side and help our relatives be happy and loved.

Skwxwú7mesh fought colonial infringement – through traditional ways.

The fight for Indigenous rights began in British Columbia around 1849. It became more structured into groups by 1916 when The Allied Indian tribes of British Columbia formed attempts to assert aboriginal rights and title. The Skwxwú7mesh chiefs (heads of families) collectively discussed maintaining rights and title and protecting the lands they saw reduced daily by settlers encroaching. The discussion meant sending a delegate to the court of England to directly ask King Edward V11 in 1906 for intervention on behalf of the Skwxwú7mesh People.

1906   Chief Joe, 53 years old, goes to London.
The Skwxwú7mesh chiefs (heads of families) collectively discussed how to assert rights and title and protect the lands they saw reduced daily by settlers encroaching. The discussion meant sending a delegate to the court of England to directly ask king Edward V11 for intervention on behalf of the Skwxwú7mesh People.

Joe Capilano began taking time off from the mill to meet Indian men fighting for Indian and Aboriginal rights. These meetings are increasingly involved in the broader issues of native rights. He then began travelling to Vancouver Island, the central interior of BC, and up the BC coast. He met with Indian leaders to promote Indian rights, land loss, and resources. He gained publicity through Vancouver newspapers because native people had lost much of their land and natural resources, fishing, and forestry. The Provincial laws constantly increased against Indians practicing the right to fish and hunt in their traditional territories.

The Siyams of Skwxwú7mesh people were talking and coming together to be organized as a people rather than the pre-existing individual families. The latter had worked together for centuries and managed the lands and resources. These Siyams – Chiefs understood the need to speak as a more prominent voice to the infringing settler society rapidly taking up space and taking land from families who had been there for centuries.

The need for the Skwxwú7mesh people to gather and be collective in speaking was critical. The people appointed Joe Capilano to support speaking for the families. *In 1906, Joe led a delegation to London, England, to meet King Edward V11. The group consisted of native elders - Secwepemc Chief Basil, Cowichan Chief Charley Isipaymit. Joe and the Chiefs he met with saved their own money for the trip. Simon Pierre of Katzie went with them as the official interpreter. William Nahanee, Alfred Jacobs, Henry Jack, and others helped draft the document for the King.*

To help increase his stature in meeting with the King, Skwxwú7mesh and Musqueam leaders, in a special ceremony, gave Joe a name that was several generations of respected leaders among the Skwxwú7mesh and Musqueam people. The name was Kiyapalanexw. The anglicized version is Capilano. So, from then, he was Joe Capilano.

The delegation said in their petition, "We have our families to keep the same as the white man, and we know how to work the like the white man as well, then why should we not have the same privileges as the white man. In addition, the petition pointed out that the aboriginal title to the land still existed.

Joe's delegation sought improved Native-White relations. They wished to remove the potlatch ban; obtain relief from hunting and fishing restrictions that inhibited their cultural and economic traditions. A significant concern included encroachment on reserved land. Governor James Douglas had promised that earmarked land was safe. However, Aboriginal people did not vote, so Indian agents did not consult them on matters affecting their lives.

There was difficulty in trying to meet the King. A newspaper company, the Morning Leader, wrote: "When His Majesty, King Edward heard how anxious the chiefs were to see him, he arranged that they should have an audience at Buckingham Palace. The King listened but did nothing. When he returned, Joe expelled the Catholic church from the Capilano reserve because the church would not support his trip to London.

Not long after becoming a chief in the late 19th century, Joe Capilano started travelling to Vancouver Island and the coast to talk to indigenous groups about what was then known as native rights. (Griffin, 2017)

1909 brings new restrictions for Skwxwú7mesh people
In 1909 the new premier Richard McBride would reiterate the province's longstanding denial of Indian Title. His quote was:

> *"Of course, it would be madness to concede to the Indians' demands; it's too late to discuss dispossessing the Redman in America."* (Mitchell, The Allied Indian Tribes of British Columbia: A study in pressure group behaviour, 1973)

In 1911, Indian Affairs amended the Indian Act to allow municipalities and companies to expropriate reserves without surrendering Indian reservations for lands, railways, and other public works. Also, a judge could move an entire Indian community from a municipality if deemed "expedient." (These changes were named after Frank Oliver, the superintendent general of Indian Affairs.) Indian Affairs would make many arbitrary changes to the Indian Act over several decades. This would be the fate of the Snauq lands of Chief August Jack Khahsalano's family. This would be the second move the Khahtsalano family would make. The first for the August Jack Khahtsalano's family was when Lord Stanley Park was renamed and created on top of the village sites such as Pa'payuk(renamed Brockton Point), Xwáýxway (Renamed Lumberman's Arch) and Chaythoos as most of the peninsula is known). (Barman, 2005) The family's relocation also meant relocating his father's remains, Khay-Tulk – from the Chaythoos resting place, near the family home. The remains were relocated to the reserve graveyard for chiefs. This was done around 1880 when the last longhouse was removed.

1913 Royal Commission in full force

Significant events occurred: amalgamation, Royal Commission on the land question, sale of Skwxwú7mesh reserve lands by Indian Affairs between 1911-and 1923. This was done without consultation or surrender of the Skwxwú7mesh People. Many tribes in BC were concerned about colonialists encroaching on their traditional territories and continued fighting for a fair settlement of their land and title rights. To resolve the so-called "Indian land question," the McKenna-McBride Royal Commission was established in 1913-1916 as a joint federal and provincial commission "to adjust the acreage of Indian reserves in British Columbia." The governments believed that the Royal Commission could settle the Indian Question and reserve size in British Columbia once and for all time. Andrew Paull acted as an Interpreter between the Skwxwú7mesh and the Royal Commission. The meetings in Vancouver had the chiefs of Skwxwú7mesh in attendance. Premier Richard McBride was the overall voice for the Indigenous peoples of British Columbia. He did not believe there were any collected tribes left living in the lower mainland area of Vancouver.

McBride spoke of the people of Skwxwú7mesh as 'Indigent and transient". The need for reserves in the Vancouver area was unnecessary, as they could not maintain even basic garbage and streets. These statements from the royal commission between McBride and Mckenna and other governing bodies of local municipalities combined to create a narrative of the Skwxwú7mesh people. The federal and provincial and municipal governments prevented the indigenous people from harvesting trees or other resources for resources to sell, and they prevented them from subsistence hunting and fishing without permission from the local government.

Skwxwú7mesh Amalgamation discussions amongst the chiefs

Skwxwú7mesh Nation chiefs began discussions for the amalgamation of its 26 reserves. Although before 1923, the Skwxwú7mesh people lived in many Indian accounts in Vancouver, Howe Sound and Skwxwú7mesh developed long-standing interconnected affiliations. At the formation of reserve land, the Joint Indian Reserve Commission gave all Skwxwú7mesh Indians the right to reside on any reserves allocated to the Skwxwú7mesh people. Headmen led them. Some headmen were the head of more than one reserve in some cases. A few more extensive reservations held meetings with a few nation members, and the committee felt a need for the Skwxwú7mesh people to unite as a larger group. Over the next seven years, Skwxwú7mesh speaking people began discussing becoming one nation. Part of the drive for the Skwxwú7mesh people to amalgamate was the Royal Commission on the land question. The Commission met with Indian bands to review reserve sizes and either enlarge or decrease reserve sizes.

Amalgamation 1923:

The headmen and committee travelled to many Skwxwú7mesh reserves to promote Amalgamation. In their travels, people said they were not interested in amalgamation. Old Skwxwú7mesh people found it hard to grasp its full implications. Some of them did not speak English or knew extraordinarily little English. The headmen questioned how their status would be affected. After Andy and some committee members had spoken to opposing chiefs, the vote passed. On July 23, 1923, 16 Skwxwú7mesh leaders and villages amalgamated into one nation. The Skwxwú7mesh Indian Band was born, and the chair of the Chiefs Council was the Superintendent of Indian Affairs from the beginning until 1985. The superintendent would decide what lands to use and how they could be used, such as through commercial development or agreements with leasing. Creating 99-year leases for businesses became a regular activity of the council.

Amalgamation would create many changes in the families of the Skwxwú7mesh people. Until then, the Skwxwú7mesh people consisted of kinship ties. Kinship ties were the most vital links uniting individuals living in various houses located in greater Vancouver, Howe Sound, and the Skwxwú7mesh Valley. The building of the Residential School in Mission Reserve in North Vancouver and a church meant that many people of the Skwxwú7mesh people had migrated to the Village of Sla7an and Capilano reserves between 1923-and 1930. The remaining villages were left most of the year. They were not abandoned but instead enforced restricted movement families from accessing their lands. The pass system was effective from 1885-to 1951. Skwxwú7mesh people never left their lands, and implemented the law by the colonial government of the day created the perfect storm for the government to reduce land size in British Columbia through several measures:

➢ Indian Act – overreaching legislation to enforce the rule of law on Indigenous people

➢ Residential school – mandatory for all indigenous children

➢ Reservation pass system – restricting movement to employment

➢ Reduced access to gainful employment the resources due to the rule of law

➢ Reduced lands to be unable to sustain through agriculture in the urban setting

➢ Encroachment from settlers arriving in significant numbers between 1854-1900

➢ The diseases reduced 75% of the Skwxwú7mesh Population between 1854-and 1900. Population went from 178,000 – 1854 to 30,000 in 1900.

➢ Enfranchisement of women and children 1876-1985

➢ Status Registration federally with Indian Affairs of all indigenous people from birth. (Unless enfranchised)

These are several reasons for the reduction of Skwxwú7mesh Land and rights. The list is not complete. It shows several areas that contributed to Skwxwú7mesh's history and decline.

Other factors at play include families of different nationalities that married and were unable to settle in other areas and became part of the Skwxwú7mesh people. These are ethnic families who immigrated through work and settlers.

The kinship group made residential mobility and social intercourse possible in Skwxwú7mesh villages. In greater Vancouver, the priests had insisted on individual homes instead of longhouses. There were new families at the Mission reserve: Spaniards, Hawaiians, Filipinos, Latin Americans, Irish, English, Germans, and Europeans of other nationalities. These families were not necessarily a part of a kinship group. They argued against joining the same political group and were convinced to vote on community decisions. At least several meetings were held in Vancouver and Skwxwú7mesh to discuss the possibilities of amalgamation and what it would mean for the community. A big part of the concerns was distributing band funds among all the communities instead of one community.

In some North Vancouver homes, the people were coerced and expected to live in modern single-family homes, in a new way of life. They bought their food and had store-bought clothing. The Catholic church kept the people organized in their homes and at church. The Chiefs in 1869 were Chief Joseph and Chief Harry, known as "Government Chief." In the early to mid-1900s, Chief Moses Joseph was the chief of the Mission Indian reserve.

In upper Skwxwú7mesh, many of the families of the Skwxwú7mesh lived in longhouses. The last longhouse in the upper Skwxwú7mesh Valley was still standing as a home until the early 1900's when the previous elders passed who lived there. The children and family had long been relocated to be near employment. The last longhouse was removed in the 1880s from the village of Xwáýxwáý (Lumberman's Arch), and families were expected to live in individual houses per the church and its imposing European societal rules. The people still hunted for food and used animal furs for clothing. Also, families followed the longhouse traditions. They held ceremonies for birth, coming of age and other ceremonial activities. Even with the differences in life, kinship ties were the most robust links uniting individuals living in the various houses located in the sixteen communities. The Skwxwú7mesh counted kinship up to six generations on both the father's and mother's sides. Equal importance was attached to kinship on both sides.

The differences in life in the communities of Upper and lower Skwxwú7mesh families contributed to the factionalism that continued for years. The leaders who promoted the Skwxwú7mesh's amalgamation wanted to explain any inequality or disagreement among the Skwxwú7mesh Tribe. The chiefs and members unanimously agreed the members and Chiefs of the reserves that attended the meetings that amalgamation was the only solution for the good government of the tribe. There was the expectation that the abolishment of ill-feeling had arisen in past transactions. (Verma, 1956)

Verma describes a conflict between the colonial concept of ownership of land and resources and First Nations people. For instance, Skwxwú7mesh people had a vague sentiment of ownership regarding clam beds, berry and root fields and hunting sites. Regarding ownership rights, community ownership was recognized, for example, fishing sites. The ownership rights were not centralized in one individual but were complex among the most comprehensive kinship group members in varying proportions. For example, a house group head was the owner of a fishing site, his brothers had a claim to use it, and a distant relative had a share of the owner's courtesy for permission to use it. The owner could permit a relative, however remote. The White concepts of ownership did not allow this sort of claim. Band members of a band were supposed to own land unburdened. However, there were demands from close kinship groups and members of other bands. But the Skwxwú7mesh continued to be guided, though to a limited extent, by their traditional concepts of ownership. People moved from one Indian band to another and settled there. In addition, bilateral descent, marriage, easy divorce, and remarriage between members of various bands and kinship groups created a situation in which each Skwxwú7mesh came to be related to every other, often in more than one way. [1]

Consequently, claims of what was supposed to be land allotted to and owned by one band became burdened with all sorts of claims of ownership from the members of other bands. Unfortunately, however, very few people kept written records of kinship. Moreover, the memory loss due to the passage of time tended to confuse the situation further.

[1] Verma talks at length and uses the Colonial term Squamish in place of Skwxwú7mesh – its unknown if Verma was aware of the Skwxwú7mesh name being the original name of the people. Verma's report is written in 1956.

The spokespeople were hurried to get agreements in place and present a unified front. Finally, in July 1923, the Skwxwú7mesh Nation signed an Amalgamation document. Since the local groups had consisted primarily of extended families, amalgamation meant a considerable change, like the political relationships of individuals with each other occurred. Most families who lived at the Mission were individual families with little or no family heads.

Indian Affairs, through the Indian Act, established an administrative office for the Chiefs to carry out legal and administrative duties. The Department of Indian Affairs, through the Indian Act, granted certain powers to the council. However, Indian Affairs chose what the band council could or could not do. Indian Affairs also made many changes to the Act before consulting the band, especially if the department enacted changes to stop the band from doing something. For example, the Indian Act forced the band to send all children aged seven to 16 to residential schools. In addition, the Indian Act provided for hereditary chiefs to administer any legal unit, such as the reserves, occupied by the combined group.

Another example is that the Skwxwú7mesh opted to appoint the senior heads of the households as their chiefs. As a result, the position became hereditary, meaning the extended family heads at amalgamation. (Verma, 1956)

As an Interpreter, Andrew Paull was becoming greatly concerned about Indian Affairs selling off many Skwxwú7mesh Indian reserves. Therefore, Skwxwú7mesh chiefs and Andrew Paull initiated amalgamation discussions through many petitions directed to the Department of Indian Affairs from 1913 to 1923. The Skwxwú7mesh people were a group of individual Skwxwú7mesh communities residing in Vancouver, Howe Sound and Upper Skwxwú7mesh. Each village had a Headman who loosely governed them. The Department of Indian Affairs administered the individual reserves separately. From the Department of Indian Affairs' point of view, it meant many changes. It meant a unified administration of all Skwxwú7mesh bands' lands. Then, a proper administration of all the funds of the Skwxwú7mesh people reserves.

Andy acted as an interpreter at these meetings and the discussions held with the Indian Agent in attendance. Andy worked as secretary to "Government' Chief Harry on Mission I.R. No. 1. In 1913, he served as a spokesman for those Skwxwú7mesh Indians who objected to the [Indian Reserve #6] sale by the False Creek band because only the people who lived at False Creek received the sale proceeds. Andrew Paull was also involved with timber sales at Cheakamus Indian reserve #11. Indian Affairs had changed the Indian Act to expropriate land for railways. In 1909, Indian Affairs arranged the sale of reserve lands allotted to Skwxwú7mesh People around the mouth of the Skwxwú7mesh River to Howe Sound, Pemberton Valley, and Northern Railway. The reserve lands around Skwxwú7mesh Island, now downtown Skwxwú7mesh, around St'á7mes and Kaẃtín, were also sold. Indian Affairs hired Andy Paull to take Skwxwú7mesh land to sell to Pacific Great Eastern Railway (PGE) to continue their work. The following Indian reserve lands, Nos. 18, 19, 20, 21, 22, 23 and 24, are to the PGE for substantial proceeds. Second, in 1922, a similar distribution method distributed significant sums from the timber sale at Cheakamus IR No. 11.

The money went to the Skwxwú7mesh reserve members in the area. Indian Affairs also worked with the Skwxwú7mesh Band to sell timber at the Seymour Reserve #2. Next, Capilano reserve #5 signed a lease to sell gravel. Finally, the Pacific Great Eastern (PGE) also took land at Capilano Indian reserve #5 and Mission reserve #1. The PGE also required a parcel of Stawamus #24.

Chief Joe Mathias of the Capilano Reserve No. 5 and Chief Harry of the Mission reserve No. 1 stated that outsiders had endeavoured him for his reservation. Ditchburn felt that they would have to move some time. It would eventually be surrendered and sold. The most unambiguous indication of the Federal Crown's willingness to contemplate removing Indian reserves from urban areas was its enactment of the *Oliver Act* in 1911. (Amended to municipalities and companies to expropriate portions of reservations without surrender for roads, railroads, and other public works. The Indian Act changes also allowed a judge to move an entire reserve away from a municipality if deemed "expedient." These amendments were also known as the Oliver Act, named after Frank, the serving superintendent general of Indian Affairs. Finally, it amended the Indian Act to Allow the Crown to purchase urban Indian reservations without the Indians' consent with judicial oversight and parliamentary approval. An example of an Indian Affairs action transaction was selling large portions of the reservations in the Skwxwú7mesh River valley to the Pacific Great Eastern Development Company. These activities or proposed activities sparked the beginning of a shift in attitude about how the Skwxwú7mesh People's reservations are enduring.

The Skwxwú7mesh people became concerned about who received the money from the sales transactions. The Department agreed to withhold the issuance until the Skwxwú7mesh completed their discussions about amalgamation.

There were at least seven meetings held to discuss amalgamation. There were chiefs and headmen at these meetings. Among other concerns, the Indian chiefs and headmen addressed the distribution of funds held in trust for the Skwxwú7mesh reserves. Only six communities out of 16, benefited from the sale of timber at Cheakamus, land sold to the PGE, gravel from the Capilano River, land expropriation by the Vancouver Harbor Commission, and sale of wood on the Seymour Indian reserve. The Nation had 28 reservations, and all 28 reservations should have benefitted from the enormous amounts of money.

Skwxwú7mesh people tried to be a united tribe in the push by Vancouver's political and business leaders in the early 1900s to advocate the surrender and sale of the False Creek reserve and the other Indian reserves around Burrard Inlet. Indian Affairs' justification for this demand was undesirable to maintain Indian reservations in an urban environment. Another rationale was that reservations were in locations that had become desirable for industrial and residential development. The province agreed to remove urban reserves and aggressively purchased the False Creek reserve in the 1913 sale. Officials of the Department of Indian Affairs appeared to accept that Vancouver's urban reservations were not desirable in Vancouver.

On the other hand, Ditchburn of Indian Affairs did not want the Skwxwú7mesh Nation to amalgamate. It would be easier for Indian Affairs to get the smaller communities of the Skwxwú7mesh People to take their land for the more significant benefit of the settler population. A united Skwxwú7mesh Band would be more challenging to remove the native land set aside for the Skwxwú7mesh people. Superintendent General Scott tried to delay the move toward amalgamation. He wrote to Andy Paull and rejected his request for amalgamation. Scot feared that the band's funds carried in the trust would be combined into one fund. Also, he wanted the Skwxwú7mesh bands separate because they lived around Burrard Inlet, with land becoming unbelievably valuable in the eyes of the colonists. Therefore, if the groups were separate, they would vote independently to sell their lands and be easier to persuade them to sell their lands.

Indian Agent Perry supported amalgamation and recommended the delay of distribution of the proceeds from the timber sale. The Superintendent of Indian Affairs rejected amalgamation because some Skwxwú7mesh People had received monies. He feared backlash from those Skwxwú7mesh People who had not shared in the distribution.

July 17, 1923, a meeting was held at the Mission reserve, the sixth meeting for amalgamation. 45 Skwxwú7mesh Indians, including all the Skwxwú7mesh chiefs, except Chief Harry of Seymour. Indian Agent Perry presided, and Andrew Paull acted as the interpreter. The Skwxwú7mesh people were getting closer to achieving amalgamation.

Andrew Paull was selected to be an interpreter for the Commission. He worked with the Skwxwú7mesh Nation chiefs to amalgamate the Skwxwú7mesh reserves into one Skwxwú7mesh Nation. A committee began meetings with various Skwxwú7mesh communities to discuss amalgamation in preparation for the Commission's visit when it would come to the Vancouver area.

Andrew Paull's involvement with Allied Tribes created some of the impetus for the Skwxwú7mesh petitions for amalgamation in 1913. In addition, Andrew Paull's knowledge of the law helped him work with the Skwxwú7mesh people. And Indian Affairs' desire to sell off other Skwxwú7mesh Reserves caused Andy to write the first proposal for amalgamation on January 20, 1913. 35 Skwxwú7mesh chiefs and band members asked for an elected council in this document.

The BC Indian Chiefs were interested in creating the Allied Indian Tribes of British Columbia. The Allied Indians formed in response to McKenna-McBride Commission. The two men who were the most prominent force behind the Allied Indian Tribes were Andrew Paull from the Skwxwú7mesh Nation and Peter Kelly from The Queen Charlotte Islands. Peter was the young leader who had made such an impression at the Victoria conference of 1911.

This amalgamation was supposed to improve the good feeling amongst the families and divide all funds from resources for all Skwxwú7mesh equally.

The level of Indian dissatisfaction on land matters continued into the early years of the 1910s. Indian peoples' hunting, fishing, and trapping activities, the free pursuit of which the Indians considered their right, became increasingly regulated by government departments. At times prosecutions occurred for breach of these regulations. Indians also complained about the shortage of pasture lands for grazing their cattle. Many Indians faced prosecution for grazing their cattle on traditional pasture lands, now leased by settlers. By this time, some Indigenous leaders had acquired a fair understanding of governmental institutions, Canadian law, and their rights under that law. They, therefore, began to explore legal avenues for presentation and redress of their grievances. In this way, the assistants came from non-Indigenous lawyers and others. They built up a strong case, supported by documents, to compel the Dominion and Provincial governments to recognize Indian title and make adequate compensation. They also agitated for a judicial decision on their claim to the Indian title. This agitation took the form of sending deputations and submitting petitions to the authorities.

1913 to 1916 A Royal Commission McKenna McBride comes to town
While Skwxwú7mesh people were trying to have their rights heard, the Rest of the Country was gearing up for the Royal Commission to deal with the "Indian Problem."

Indian dissatisfaction with land matters continued into the early years of the 1900s. Indian peoples' hunting, fishing, and trapping activities, the free pursuit of which the Indians considered their right, became increasingly regulated by government departments. At times prosecutions occurred for breach of these regulations. Indians also complained about the shortage of pasture lands for grazing their cattle. Many Indians faced prosecution for grazing their cattle on traditional pasture lands, now leased by settlers. By this time, some Indigenous leaders had acquired a fair understanding of governmental institutions, Canadian law, and their rights under that law. They, therefore, began to explore legal avenues for presentation and redress of their grievances. In this way, the assistants came from lawyers and other non-indigenous people. They built up a strong case, supported by documents, to compel the Dominion and Provincial governments to recognize Indian title and make adequate compensation. They also agitated for a judicial decision on their claim to the Indian title. This agitation took the form of sending deputations and submitting petitions to the authorities. For instance, Chief Joe Capilano led a delegation to meet the King in England in 1906. This meeting is discussed elsewhere in this paper.

Several deputations of Indians presented their grievances to the Dominion Prime Minister when he visited British Columbia in 1910. In the same year, a delegation of Friends of the Indians waited upon the Prime Minister of British Columbia.

In 1911, Indian Chiefs met in Victoria. Two things happened: The First Nations of BC met to work together to organize protests, and the federal and provincial governments realized that what they called the "Indian Problem" was not going away. So, they decided to form a Royal Commission to resolve the problem. The federal and provincial governments called it the McKenna-McBride Commission, composed of federal minister McKenna and provincial premier McBride. The Commission also included Andrew Paul.

In 1913, the Federal Government Royal Commission appointed a Royal Commission. Andrew worked as an interpreter for the Royal Commission, formed to resolve the "Indian reserve question. During this time, Andrew also worked part-time for the Vancouver Province newspaper. He also, on a part-time basis, published two newspapers. He wanted to reach the Indian and non-Indian people about the concerns of Indian people through publishing articles on land claims, employment issues, and education.

The Prime Minister issued An Order-in-Council, passed in 1914, which proposed that the Exchequer Court of Canada decision on the condition that if the Indians won the case, they would accept the Royal Commission's findings on the reserve question. And get "benefits granted for the extinguishment of title following the past in usage of the Crown. However, Indians refused to accept any such condition in advance, so a court about Indian title never happened.

They were to visit each First Nations communities in BC, in order to consult with the people about the amount of land they required, and assign additional reserves. Some bands refused to meet with the Commission, while others made presentations and reinforced their desire for treaties. The commission did make new reserves, but it also removed valuable land from certain reservations. (Government of Canada. 1913-1916). These lands became known as cut-off lands, and most of them were in urban areas where the property had come to have significant economic potential, such as Skwxwú7mesh lands. The land was in Greater Vancouver, which became the third-largest city in Canada.

The Commission removed the reservation land because the colonial people did not want Indian people to own valuable land. It would take the Skwxwú7mesh people another 80 years to win the fight for the value of the land removed. One such settlement agreed upon by the Skwxwú7mesh people was 92.5 million dollars. These were the Kitsilano lands settled in 1996.

The Dominion Government confirmed the Commission's report on July 19, 1924. It was a final adjustment of all Indian questions between the Dominion and the Province. Before securing the information, however, the Dominion Government negotiated with the Indians to set some reasonable compensation, which the Dominion Government might supply to settle the question of Indian title out of court. But the Dominion felt that Indian demands were too extravagant, and the Dominion Government dropped the plan.

The Indians refused to accept the findings of the Commission. They objected to the Commission's terms of reference from the very start. The McKenna-McBride Agreement provided that the Commission's report would finally adjust the Indian question if agreed to by both governments. And as final adjustment would logically preclude the opening of inquiry of an Indian title by ignoring it. However, the Commission was not supposed to deal with it under its terms of reference.

In 1913, Duncan Campbell Scott, Department of Indian Affairs, had now attained a position where he created the departmental policy and advised politicians on drafting new legislation. Scott was an influential bureaucrat whose intentions were for his department to complete the total assimilation of Indians into mainstream Canadian society. He felt that the Indian people would have a happy future as an enfranchised people in the general population. Scott planned to make enfranchisement a reality by ensuring that intermarriage continued to happen. He also encouraged the Indian people to get higher education and then they must enfranchise. These actions would finally overcome the lingering traces of native custom and tradition.

In 1911, Indian Affairs amended the Indian Act to allow municipalities and companies to expropriate reserves without surrendering roads, railways, and other public works. Also, a judge could move an entire Indian community from a city if it were deemed "expedient." Over the years, Indian Affairs would make many arbitrary decisions to change the Indian Act. These changes were made to accommodate other groups, such as when the war was over.

The soldiers returned home; in 1918, the Indians remained wards of the federal government, so they were not treated the same as Canadians as returning soldiers. For instance, the federal government created the Soldier Settlement Act, which provided land to veterans. The government removed reserve land for non-Indigenous soldiers under the plan. The amount taken was Eighty-five thousand eight hundred forty-four acres.

Discussions on Amalgamation continue.
Significant events occurred: amalgamation; Royal Commission on the land question; Indian Affairs sold many Skwxwú7mesh Indian lands between 1911-and 1923.

First, with other tribes in BC, the Skwxwú7mesh people were concerned about colonialists encroaching on their traditional territories and continued fighting for a fair settlement of their land and title rights. Second, to conclusively resolve the so-called "Indian land question," the McKenna-McBride Royal Commission was established as a joint federal and provincial commission "to adjust the acreage of Indian reserves in British Columbia." The governments believed that if additional First Nations received more reserves, they would be satisfied. Andrew Paull acted as an Interpreter for Royal Commission. (Government of Canada. 1913-1916)

Two, Skwxwú7mesh Nation chiefs were considering the amalgamation of its 26 reserves. Before 1923, the Skwxwú7mesh people lived in many Indian reservations in Vancouver; Howe Sound and Skwxwú7mesh developed long-standing interconnected affiliations. At the formation of reserve land, the Joint Indian Reserve Commission gave all Skwxwú7mesh Indians the right to reside on any reserves allocated to the Skwxwú7mesh people. Headmen led them. Some headmen were the head of more than one reserve in some cases. A few more extensive reservations held meetings with a few band members, and the committee felt a need for the Skwxwú7mesh people to unite as a larger group. Over the next seven years, Skwxwú7mesh speaking bands began discussions to become one band. Part of the drive for the Skwxwú7mesh people to amalgamate was the Royal Commission on the land question. The Commission met with Indian bands to review reserve sizes and either enlarge or decrease reserve sizes.

From 1914 –to 1918, Canada enters World War 1 - I (a break to amalgamation talks?)
Canada became involved because it was part of the British Empire. When Great Britain declared war on Germany in August of 1914, its empire did well. In addition, Britain had colonies in many countries. Thus, the war became a world war.

Canada's contribution of volunteers included at least 4,000 First Nations soldiers. For some, it was a culture shock. The men had to learn discipline; this was difficult; military life demanded strict discipline. The volunteers consisted of soldiers, nurses, and civilians. They became part of integrated units. The Skwxwú7mesh people list at least five people who volunteered to go to war. They are:

Jim Daniels
Andy Naturall. He served as a sniper/gunner with 90% accuracy.
Albert Newman
Charles Newman
George Newman. He served as a machine gunner in France and Germany.
On the home front, Skwxwú7mesh band members raised money for the war effort and made significant financial contributions to the soldiers to help the costs of the war effort.

When the war was over and the soldiers returned home, Canada remained indifferent to the First Nations' concerns. In 1918, The Indians remained wards of the federal government, so they were not treated the same as Canadians as returning soldiers. For instance, the federal government created the Soldier Settlement Act, which provided land to veterans. The government removed reserve land for non-Indigenous soldiers under the plan. The amount taken was Eighty-five thousand eight hundred forty-four acres.

1918   Worldwide, Spanish flu occurs.
During this time, the Skwxwú7mesh people lost many people. My uncle Bill and others said that people were dying in great numbers. The people helping with the crisis took the dead to the graveyard in wheelbarrows. There was no time for proper burials. My grandmother and many women worked tirelessly to nurse the sick and dying. At the end of the epidemic, Cecilia died from exhaustion. The nation's population became significantly decreased.

1920:
In 1920 Parliament passed an Act to implement the recommendations of the McKenna-McBride Royal Commission Report on the land question. Andy Paull and Peter Kelley of The Allied Indian Tribes continued to resist. In 1923, a gathering of most of the Indian tribes in British Columbia came together in Skwxwú7mesh Reserve 1, North Vancouver and four Skwxwú7mesh

representatives participated in it. At this meeting, two Indian factions formed an independent party called the Allied Indian Tribes of British Columbia. Andrew Paul, Secretary of the Skwxwú7mesh Council, as secretary of the Allied Indian Tribes and Peter Kelley gave evidence before the Special Committee of the Senate and House of Commons in 1926 to support the claim for Indian title. Before the Special Committee, Andrew Paull was a witness to amending the Indian Act in 1946. The Allied Indian Tribes petitioned the government. In August 1923, federal officials made an almost unprecedented visit to British Columbia to meet with the Allied Indian Tribes. Interior Minister Charles Stewart (responsible for Indian Affairs) and Scott, Deputy Superintendent of Indian Affairs, met with the executive of the Allied Indian Tribes, including Andrew Paull, Peter Kelly, and twelve other leaders. As was later written, this visit "revealed "the power of unity that existed among all the BC Indian Tribes at that time." (Government of Canada. 1913-1916)

At the opening of the meeting, Kelly put an old issue to rest. Just as in earlier times, an assumption existed that non-native people supported First Nations people when political action happened. With the Allied Tribes, AE O'Meara, the lawyer, received blame for political action taken by the First Nations people.

Peter Kelly presented their case, and Stewart promised to take it before the cabinet. However, it required another petition for any action to happen. Finally, in 1926 a Special Joint Committee of the Senate and the House of Commons investigated land claims and Aboriginal titles in British Columbia. The official record of this committee includes documents submitted in evidence that compile all the work by various First Nations groups and leaders since 1875 and (Allied Indian Tribe) the testimony given by witnesses. Today the paper provides an excellent summary of the land claims struggle for researchers. The outcome, however, was far from satisfactory. The committee recommended a yearly payment of $100,000 to provide technical education, hospital care and medicine, agriculture promotion, irrigation, projects, and nothing else. These were all areas in which the government already had an obligation to provide. However, as Kelly noted, the idea of the grant did prove something.

The grant of $100,000 indirectly recognizes the validity of the Indian land question of British Columbia. The British Columbia Indians claim that if their title to lands of BC were without foundation, why would there be the necessity of a $100,000 annual payment 'instead of an annuity. Thus, the grant deviously admits the actuality of the Indian land claims of British Columbia.

The Allied Indian Tribes successfully made changes or stopped the enforcement of some sections of the Indian Act. The success of the Allied Tribes caused Indian Affairs to make another change. In 1929, The new law made it a criminal act for First Nations people to try to achieve recognition of Aboriginal title or to pursue their Aboriginal rights. It was illegal to raise money to pursue land claims; it was unlawful for people to meet to talk about land claims. Because of these new restrictions, Indian people across BC had to find new ways of continuing their struggle to recognize Rights and Entitlement.

In 1927, Andrew Paull went to Ottawa to represent the Allied Tribes of BC and the Skwxwú7mesh Nation. They sought permission to decide on an Indian title by reference to a court. The same year a Special Committee of the Senate and House of Commons was appointed to inquire into the claims outlined in the petition. The Committee examined the evidence and decided that British Columbia was conquered territory. (The occasional clashes of a local nature between a few groups of Indians and non-indigenous settlers were evidence of conquest) and that any Indian title did not burden the Crown's right to land. The Indians received full opportunity to test their claims in court, which they did not do. (According to the Committee, of course, Indigenous people couldn't go to court without any ability at the fairness of the Legal system to remediate their claims) The Committee, therefore, recommended that the matter be finally closed. Instead of paying annuities as done in many other Canadian provinces, the Committee recommended that $100,000 be expended annually for education, medical care, agriculture, stock raising and irrigation projects for Indians. The Indians, of course, were anything but satisfied with the recommendations of the committee. A trail of bitterness was left behind. The purpose was to testify at a special parliament committee to discuss ongoing concerns over the McKenna McBride Royal Commission. (Government of Canada. 1913-1916)

Included in the education of the Skwxwú7mesh people discussions were the broader issue of Aboriginal Rights and title. In Ottawa, a Special Committee on the Indian Act held hearings to consider changing the Indian Act. At the same time, federal and provincial governments were attempting to settle the land issues arising out of the McKenna-McBride Commission. 1923, the Allied Indian Tribes met with national politicians and bureaucrats to discuss ongoing concerns over the McKenna McBride Royal Commission. They tried to convince the governments to reject the Commission's findings and settle the broader issue of Aboriginal Rights and Title. Four years later, the Special Joint Committee of the House of Commons and the Senate on Indian Affairs heard representations from many organizations, including the Allied Tribes. They submitted a petition in June 1926, resulting in a Special Committee of the Senate and House of Commons to inquire into the Claims of the Allied Indian Tribes of British Columbia. The committee concluded "that the claims of the Indians were not well-founded and that no Aboriginal title, as alleged, had ever existed." In 1927 Canada amended the Indian Act to make it illegal to obtain funds or legal counsel to advance Aboriginal Title cases. (Mitchell, Allied Indian Tribes of British Columbia: in pressure group behaviour. 1977) The act ended the Allied Tribes' hope of hearing a chance at the Privy Council in London, and the Allied Tribes dissolved. Indigenous resistance moved underground.

Duncan Campbell Scott, "I want to get rid of the Indian problem. I do not think this country should protect a class of people who can stand alone continuously. That is my whole point. I do not want to pass into the citizens' class, people who are paupers. (1920-1927 Indian Act) But after 100 years of being in close contact with civilization, it is enervating to the individual or a band to during these discussions," Scott was concerned about the fact that Indian people across Canada were continuing in their efforts to keep on pressing for dealing with the issues of land claims and aboriginal rights. To stop these demands, he had the Indian Act amended to read that, under section 141, it was illegal to "raise money from any Indian or Indians to prosecute any claim against the government." DIA used the Indian Act to threaten fines or imprisonment if they pursued their case to the Privy Council in London.

Amalgamation papers are finalized and "approved" in 1923:

On September 26, 1923, Scott issued instructions to consolidate the Skwxwú7mesh accounts.
The Amalgamation was official on July 23, 1923, and The Squamish Indian band was now the
legal name of the Skwxwú7mesh people.

RETYPED FOR EASIER READING

SQUAMISH NATION OF INDIANS

NORTH VANCOUVER

BRITISH COLUMBIA.

Dr. Duncan C. Scott   July 23rd, 1923
Deputy Superintendent General of Indian Affairs.

Sir:

We the undersigned on behalf of the Squamish Indians beg
leave to respectfully convey the prayer of the Squamish Indians for
your consideration and approval.

In preamble we take the liberty to acquaint you with the
fact that the Squamish Nation of Indians have had under
consideration for the past eight years the question of the
amalgamation of the several bands of the tribe and after a series
of meetings recently, during which we considered and digested the
question of amalgamation and with a view of illuminating for all
time to come any inequality or disagreement among the Squamish
Tribe. It was unanimously agreed by the members and Chiefs of the
under mentioned reserves, that the amalgamation of the several
Bands is the only solution for the good government of the tribe,
which would have as an ultimate result the abolishment of ill
feeling that has arisen in past transactions, and which we know
will henceforth bring about a brotherly feeling among each and
every member of the Squamish people.

The amalgamation of Skwxwú7mesh people: documents provided by Chief Donald Mathias

- 2 -

It has also been agreed that the several funds of the Squamish Indians held in trust for them by the Government be consolidated into one fund and that any future disbursement of money be equally divided among the Squamish people.

With a view of properly conducting the affairs of the Squamish Indians we have unanimously agreed to have a council to transact the affairs of our people in co-operation with the Indian Department, said council to be composed of all the chiefs of the Squamish Nation of Indians, and we may say that said council has met with the approval of every chief of the Squamish Indians and the people.

The above is the true and sincere desire of the Squamish people for their future welfare, and we are thankful in having the honour of meeting you in person, to most sincerely pray that you approve of the amalgamation of the Squamish Indians, and the consolidation of _____.

So further and more respectfully pray that you approve of the council and give due recognition of chiefs of the Squamish Indians to act as a council for the Squamish people, and we hope that any representations that the council may make in the future will receive a sympathetic and attentive hearing from the Government, and especially the Department of Indian Affairs to whom we look for protection, guidance and assistance in the good government of our affairs.

That power be granted the council of chiefs to enact bylaws for the good government of the members.

Page 2 of amalgamation letter – provided by Chief Donald Mathias

- 3 -

It is the desire of the people that the superintendent general or his deputy would by his most generous consideration to such representation and recommendation as council of tribe may from time to time to make, having in view the improvement or development of any of its reserves and the expenditure of tribal funds for this purpose. The council will give due regard to the practice of economy and will endeavour to make restriction of foolish or extravagant nature.

We beg to say that the above are the principle requirements of the Squamish people, and we again say that we will ever pray for the amalgamation of the Squamish Indians and the consolidation of the funds; and that in our opinion the only and proper manner of administering the affairs of our people is through a council of the chiefs in co-operation with the Department, and again pray that you give our council recognition, to this we will ever pray, And we hereby affix our signatures and marks to certify to the above, on behalf of the Squamish Nation of Indians we are humbly but respectfully,

Page 32 provided by Chief Donald Mathias

Pictures are courtesy of Chief Donald Mathias of Capilano Indian Band

Dirty Thirties

During the 1930s, Canada and the whole world experienced the Great Depression, when there were unprecedented levels of poverty and unemployment due to unemployment. Although in non-Indian reserve populations, the amounts were 40%, unemployment in the Indian reserves was closer to 80%. Indian women who lived on Indian reserves were not counted. Nor were women who stayed home to raise families were not counted in the statistics, nor were people who did not search for work. Also, people, such as longshoremen who would show up at worksites hoping to get day jobs, would not be included. Jobs were difficult to find. Vancouver became home to thousands of unemployed men who came to Vancouver to work. These men were willing to work for meagre wages to have a job. The wage rate for unskilled labour was $.40 an hour. Skwxwú7mesh men found it increasingly difficult to find work with so much work available to transients. Men were increasingly employed more often than women because men were the family supporter and needed more than women.

Among the few women in the labour force, layoffs were less common in white-collar jobs. Instead, women found work found in light manufacturing. However, there was a widespread demand to limit families to one paid position, employment if their husband was employed.

In 1936, another amendment was directed to all Indian Agents to allow Indian agents to control band council meetings and cast a deciding vote in case of a tie.[39] The Indian Act determined what Indian bands could be allowed to do.

Skwxwú7mesh homemakers did their best to feed and clothe their families by buying fresh fruit and vegetables in bulk for home canning. In addition, they were able to secure fresh salmon for home canning and smoking. The women either had their smokehouses or used a neighbour's. Cheap foods were used, such as soups, beans, and noodles. With salmon, they could make sandwiches and or soup.

1946 a special parliamentary committee.
As president of the NAIB, Andrew Paull stood before the Special Joint Committee of the Senate and House of Commons. The committee that was appointed to examine and consider the Indian Act. 27 June,1946 (he stood, ignoring an invitation by the committee chair, who asked him if he would rather sit down), is compelling reading, revealing a well-spoken and highly prepared orator, despite his self-deprecating remarks requesting the committee to "disregard [his] inability to speak and [his] lack of command of the English language." (Edwards, 2010)

In his plea for greater Aboriginal involvement in the Indian government and for the

Government of Canada to recognize that it violated the treaties, Paull used the literature of

the treaties and subsequent legal studies to make his point, illustrating and effectively

reminding them that the First Nations people who signed the treaties with the British crown

and Canadian government were acting as sovereign powers and recognized as such

by the Euro-Canadians involved:
I have read in the evidence of Mr. T.R.L. MacInnes (Secretary, Indian
Affairs Branch) that the Indian had nothing to give when he signed
the treaty because he had not colonized the country. Now, we can give
you plenty of decisions to contradict that argument, but we know that
you are men of learning, and I do not think it will be necessary to do
that. That is why I did not bring the books here, but we can give you
decisions to contradict the statements made by Mr. MacInnes.
In 1947, Andrew Paull spoke at the Special Joint Committee hearings on the Indian Act. He
revealed a consistent theme of his advocacy as he stressed the need to improve Aboriginal
education: "The Hon. Mr. Crerar, I can give you the answer in one word: education.' Because
the Indian is educated, he can fight for himself from his difficulties. He will not feel an
inferiority complex. If he has an education, he will think that he is equal to anybody. That was
the answer I gave to Hon. Mr. Crerar. (Canada, Parliament, Special Joint Committee of the
Senate and the House of Commons Appointed to Continue and Complete the Examination
and Consideration of the Indian Act, *Minutes of Proceedings and Evidence,* no. 18. Ottawa:
Edmund Cloutier, Printer to the King's Most Excellent Majesty, 1947. 887) Andrew Paull
advocated for libraries to be available to Indian reserves to improve literacy, but his pleas fell
on deaf ears. On the one hand, the federal government and missionaries wanted Indian
children to be educated to support the Canadian economy. They did not wish young

Aboriginal intellectuals to challenge the dominant Euro-Canadians. Thus, little thought, effort, or funding was put into literacy programs or placing schools or public libraries in Aboriginal communities. (Titley, 1986)

The 1950s

Indigenous persons could lose status under the Act in a variety of ways, including the following:

- marrying a man who was not a status Indian
- enfranchisement - Until 1947, Indigenous persons could not have Indian status and Canadian citizenship.
- having a father or husband who becomes enfranchised
- having at the age of 21 a mother and paternal grandmother who did not have status before marriage
- being born out of wedlock to a mother with class and a father without status.

These provisions interfered with the matrilineal cultures of many First Nations. Children were innate to the mother's clan and people and gained their belonging in the lineage from her family. Often property and hereditary leadership passed through the maternal line. In addition, the 1876 Indian Act maintained that Indigenous women with status who married status Indigenous men would, in the event of divorce, be unable to regain their Indian rights to the band they registered in. these changes occurred because the Act enforced the patrilineal descent principle required to determine an individual's eligibility.

The 1950s for the Status of Women

Status Indian women can vote in band elections. Attempts to pursue land claims and the use of religious ceremonies (such as potlatches or Dinners, Sundance's, longhouse, sweat lodges and all ceremonial practices) are allowed and further amended for the compulsory enfranchisement of First Nations women married to non-status men (including Métis, Inuit, and non-status Indian and non-Aboriginal men), thus causing them to lose their status denying Indian status to any children from the marriage. The act further added a clause to say that she could not register the second-generation female child.

Council now consisted of hereditary chiefs, some nominated based on kinship, and some were councillors, elected through secret ballot based on adult suffrage. Membership is supposed to last until the death or resignation of the member. However, there is a provision for suspension or dismissal on being convicted of an offence.

In 1952, The Indian Act, Paragraphs 80-85, specified the legal powers and jurisdiction of the Band Council.

The council is roughly as extensive as some local or municipal governments. However, unlike the latter, extraordinarily little power rests with the Band Council. The Minister in charge of Indian Affairs can disallow any by-laws passed by the Band Council within 40 days after a copy goes forward to the Minister.

Matters relating to land issues form a significant part of the discussions of the Skwxwú7mesh council. Requests for removal of gravel, timber sale, grant of a right of way, lease or sale of land are everyday items that form the plan. When approved by the council, the sale of land must go to a general meeting of the Band for approval.

The sale of land is a central political question among the Skwxwú7mesh. People have strong emotions, are even sometimes contradictory feelings from the same individuals. On the other hand, a person might want to sell the land, but he has more people to worry about for their future security. Also, there is a feeling that due to industrial development, the land prices are rising, and that would be sound business sense to wait. Council now consisted of hereditary chiefs, some nominated based on kinship, and some were councillors, elected through secret ballot based on adult suffrage. Membership is supposed to last until the death or resignation of the member.

INAC drove governing 1956

The Squamish Indian Band council of 1956 was roughly as extensive as some local or municipal governments. However, unlike the latter, extraordinarily little power rests with the Band Council. The Minister in charge of Indian Affairs can disallow any by-laws passed by the Band Council within forty days after a copy goes forward to the Minister. (Verma, 1956)

The Governing came from Council, which came from INAC Superintendent forming the new Skwxwú7mesh house group, the smallest and closest local, kinship, political and economic unit.

For instance, the Mission reserve now has people living there that do not belong to a house group. New families have moved there because men married Skwxwú7mesh wives and could live at the Mission reserve with their Skwxwú7mesh wives and families. Also, the grown children established their own homes, with the house group consisting only of the husband, wife, and children. (Verma, 1956)

Matters relating to land issues form a significant part of the discussions of the Skwxwú7mesh council. Requests for removal of gravel, timber sale, grant of a right of way, lease or sale of land are everyday items that form the plan. When approved by the council, the sale of land must go to a general meeting of the Band for approval. (Verma, 1956)

The sale of land is a central political question among the Skwxwú7mesh. People have strong emotions, are even sometimes contradictory feelings from the same individuals. Several conflicting attitudes exist on the same subject. A band member wants cash for the sale of the land. On the other hand, some people worry about their future security. Also, there is a feeling that due to industrial development, the land prices are rising, and that would be sound business sense to wait. (Verma, 1956)

All the above statements from the 1956 thesis by Behari Verma show a governing structure entirely created and imposed by the Department of Indian Affairs. The superintendent followed this governing structure as the Chair of the council until 1985 when the "self-governing" models were implemented. These policies and directives are all driven by the government's ability to manage and control the monies of the Skwxwú7mesh peoples. The model now being imposed on the modern-day Council – created by the Government of Indigenous Services and the Newly formed Squamish Nation Corporation has developed a governing structure that no longer involves the input or decisions of the people and families of Skwxwú7mesh people. The people have been renamed Squamish, and the policy and money flow to the registered corporation of the Squamish, which redistributes the funds through a series of programs and salaries designed to care for less than 10% of the membership populations of the "Squamish" Skwxwú7mesh people today.

1959   St. Paul's Indian Residential School is ended.

The school is torn down and set on fire. When it was first ready for occupation, Sister Amy was one of the nuns who first came to the school. She was here to see the destruction of the school. She recalled her years as a teacher at St. Paul's Indian residential school. It was painful for her to see the building burn because of her many years of caring for the young children at the school. Sister Amy sometimes wondered what happened to the girls when they left school. Her eyes were filled with tears as memories flowed through her mind. Sister also remembered that some mothers who sent their daughters to the school had been former students. The flames of the fire were dying down. Sister did not realize how long she had stood there. The school grounds became the site for the future St. Thomas Aquinas high school. The new school authorities agreed to allow a percentage of its students to be First Nations high school pupils to recognize the first school as a residential school for Indian students.

1959   St. Paul's Indian Day School opens
The Skwxwú7mesh nation builds a new school two blocks east of the old school. It became a day school only, no more residential school...

1964 Hawthorn Report

In 1964, the Department of Indian Affairs commissioned Dr. Harry Hawthorn to study the contemporary situation of Indians in Canada. The report was to help Jean Chretien and Prime Minister Pierre Trudeau develop a paper to delete the Department of Indian Affairs. Before doing this, Chretien needed to know what the state of the Indian people of Canada was. Hawthorn hired a team across Canada to do the work to do a report. He had a free hand to develop the information.

The team learned about the residential schools and the fate of the children who lived in the schools. Hawthorn concluded that Aboriginal peoples were Canada's most disadvantaged and marginalized population. They were "citizens minus."   They learned about the poor state of the Indian reserves. They learned about the health problems of the Indian people, their nutritional problems, inadequate housing, inadequate plumbing, and poor finances of the people.

In their report, Hawthorn recommended that the residential schools be shut down because they left students unprepared for participation in the contemporary economy.

Hawthorne's report recommended independence from the federal government's controls exercised through the Indian Act. However, the Indian people would require programs to help them take over governing themselves. Instead, Chretien and Pierre Elliott Trudeau created a document that would eliminate the Department of Indian Affairs and its controls, including Indian reserves and programs. They found a way to relieve themselves of the problems of the Indian people. There are no more residential schools, no more education funding for Indian people, no more housing needs to care about, and everything to come under the provinces. In five years, Indian reserve lands would be owned outright and available for sale by people. No more land claims to be concerned about.

To this end, the white paper proposed to

- Eliminate Indian status
- Dissolve the Department of Indian Affairs within five years
- Abolish the Indian Act
- Convert reserve land to private property that can be sold by the band or its members
- Transfer responsibility for Indian affairs from the federal government to the province and integrate these services into those provided to other Canadian citizens
- Provide funding for economic development
- Appoint a commissioner to address outstanding land claims and gradually terminate existing treaties

The federal government commissioned UBC Professor Harry B. Hawthorn to complete a study on the current state of Indigenous peoples in Canada. Hawthorn and his team's report survey the "Contemporary Indians of Canada's Economic, Political, Educational Needs and Policies," published in 1966, remains a must-read for people interested in studying Indigenous people.

Hawthorn essentially concluded that Indigenous peoples in Canada were not treated fairly and were generally at a disadvantage. Hawthorn noted the impact the residential school system had on creating the poor conditions for Indigenous peoples. Accordingly, he recommended improving Indigenous peoples' rights and the end of the forced residential schools.

The federal government used the report as a basis for its development of the White Paper.

1969 the White Paper

Pierre Trudeau, Prime Minister of Canada and his Minister of Indian Affairs, Jean Chrétien, were about to unleash another round of supreme changes to the Indian Act that would rouse the Indian people of Canada and non-Indian people. It was called the White Paper (officially called the Statement of the Government of Canada on Indian policy).

The paper, written without prior discussion with Canada's First Nation people, proposed sweeping changes to the Indian Act, dissolving the Act. The Indian Affairs department documents to be abolished and the treaties repealed. Indigenous status people of Canada would come under provincial government jurisdiction. There would be no Indian reserve land meaning that the native land would be private property. The federal government would abolish any special programs or considerations allowed to First Nations people under previous legislation. The Government saw the factors to further separate Indian peoples from Canadian citizens. Before bringing the White Paper to Parliament, Pierre's government commissioned a study of "THE CONTEMPORARY INDIANS OF CANADA Economic, Political, Educational Needs and Policies." (Hawthorn, Cairns, & Tremblay, 1966)

People researching the Skwxwú7mesh people still refer to this report in recent years. The document became the basis for the White Paper.

Indian people became more united across Canada against the Department of Indian Affairs and its inhumane treatment of Indian people. The White Paper was seen as a further attempt by Indian Affairs to assimilate the people.

An organization called Red Power drew more and more people to support them. Skwxwú7mesh people started a train full of young people to head to Ottawa to protest Indian Affairs. People boarded the train on its eastern journey as it travelled across Canada. In Ottawa, the people took over a vacant buildings and occupied it for months. Indian organizations in Ottawa collected food and other supplies for the protestors. They also raised money to assist people in The White Paper when reviewed by Indigenous and non-Indigenous people in 1969, caused by widespread anger and opposition. It did not look like anything that Indian people had been consulted about. The White Paper was created without any input about its decisions.

The Indigenous people were invited in May 1969 for consultation, and a month later, the White Paper was produced. The document was a betrayal. Land claims in BC were ignored, which meant that the BC's provincial government did not have to deal with the problem. Indian people would have to deal with a complete alternation in life. (Gibson. 2009. P.47) Harold Cardinal, a Cree leader of the Indian Association of Alberta, referred to the White Paper as a "thinly disguised program of extermination through assimilation" in his bestselling 1969 book the *Unjust Society*, which attacked the premise that society treated its Aboriginal population like Canada did could be considered "just." "Despite all government attempts to convince Indians to accept the white paper, their efforts will fail because Indians understand that the path outlined by the Department of Indian Affairs through its mouthpiece, the Honorable Mr. Chretien, leads directly to cultural genocide. We will not walk this path. Indian people would be equal with all Canadians by eliminating Indian as a special legal status and Aboriginal peoples simply as citizens with the same rights, opportunities, and responsibilities as other Canadians. P. Trudeau envisioned a just society; his government proposed repeal legislation considered discriminatory. In this view, the Indian Act was discriminatory because it applied only to Aboriginal peoples and not to Canadians in general. The white paper stated that removing the unique legal status established by the Indian Act would "enable the Indian people to be free—free to develop Indian cultures in an environment of legal, social and economic equality with other Canadians." (Cardinal, 1969)

1970s Skwxwú7mesh People
The nation started upgrading classes for its members to complete the Dogwood diploma. In addition, funds were available for The Skwxwú7mesh membership to take workshops in arts and crafts classes.

Cultural and Spiritual Revival
Culture and Spiritual revival began openly. The Potlatch ban law was repealed in 1951. The repeal meant that nearly 71 years passed since the potlatches and ceremonies of our people would be legal to practice again. The building of Long Houses openly on Skwxwú7mesh lands came after 1951. However, the teachings, oral transmission and storytelling would take decades to revive. The first speakers of the language were few. Chief Louis Miranda was working actively with universities and organizations to preserve Language.

The creation of the Skwxwú7mesh Language book would be his life's work in safeguarding Skwxwú7mesh Language.

The ceremonies and Lodges were much longer in coming back to the community. The backlash of Colonial Settler values impacted any prior contact teachings and ways of being of The Skwxwú7mesh People. A few families had personally preserved the longhouse practices such as songs, dances, and Rites of Passage. The landscape and communities had grown up and annihilated most traces of the original lodges, Long Houses, sweat lodges, and other sacred places. Stanley Park was now commerce of World Colonial view of what a Park is to be presented. Stanly Park was the Home of the Skwxwú7mesh families, who are now existing Skwxwú7mesh nation members today. The many Skwxwú7mesh families occupied these lands for centuries. The remnants of the people still exist under the ground and in the old-growth cedars that still show the old scars of Cedar bark harvesting and midge piles buried under the Aquarium and Lumberman's arch. The original name of this place is Xwáýxwáý – the place where the masks are born is the loose translation. The home of the masks. Those masks are the spirits of our ancestors and the direct line to connect to our generations of ancestors. The interruption of the Potlatch law impacted internal families and how they would begin to accept the true history of the Skwxwú7mesh people. The ceremonies started returning in forms such as the Longhouse built on Capilano reserve and the Sweat lodges in the last standing cedars along the railways on Welch Road. The return of these open practices was met with much opposition, and very few of the Skwxwú7mesh accepted these ways. However, they were able to practice in the open.

Loss of status before 1985 amendments
The federal government used enfranchisement to terminate a person's Indian status and confer full Canadian citizenship. Enfranchisement was a vital feature of the Canadian federal government's assimilation policies regarding Aboriginal peoples. Voluntary enfranchisement was introduced in the Gradual Civilization Act of 1857 and [sic] assumed that Aboriginal people would be willing to surrender their legal and ancestral identities for the "privilege" of gaining full Canadian citizenship and assimilating into Canadian society. Individuals or entire bands could enfranchise. If a man with a family is enfranchised, his wife and children would automatically be enfranchised.

However, significantly few Aboriginal people or groups were willing to abandon their cultural and legal identities, as anticipated by the colonial authorities. Enfranchisement would become legally compulsory with the Indian Act of 1876, which stood until 1951. Over time, Aboriginal people have been enfranchised for serving in the Canadian armed forces, gaining a university education, leaving reserves for long periods – for instance, for employment – and, for Aboriginal women, if they married non-Indian men or if their [sic] husbands died or abandoned them. Before 1985, Indigenous persons could lose status under the Act in a variety of ways, including the following:

- marrying a man who was not a status Indian. Skwxwú7mesh women received some compensation, about 10% of band revenue. She could never return to her band if her husband deserted her. She lost her Indian ancestry. The women became Canadian citizens and the nationality of their husbands. An example, Barbara Wyss became Swiss Canadian by law. The women became further separated from their communities physically, geographically, socially, spiritually, psychologically, and emotionally.

- Enfranchisement - Until 1947, Indigenous persons could not have Indian status and Canadian citizenship.

- Any Indians who obtained a university degree and became professionals such as doctors or lawyers automatically lost their status.

- If status Indian joined armed services

- having a father or husband who becomes enfranchised

- having at the age of 21 a mother and paternal grandmother who did not have status before marriage

- being born out of wedlock to a mother with status and a father who did not have Indian status.

These provisions interfered with the matrilineal cultures of many First Nations. Children were born to the mother's clan, and people gained their belonging in the lineage from her family. Often property and hereditary leadership passed through the maternal line.

In addition, the 1876 Indian Act maintained that Indigenous women with status who married non-status lost their status. In divorce, Indigenous men would be unable to regain their status in their band. The Indian Act's enforcement of the patrilineal descent principle is required to determine an individual's eligibility for Indian status. As individuals, Indigenous women were not eligible for status or the ability to transfer status to their children. Indian status could only be reacquired or transferred legally by proof of an Indigenous father or marriage to a husband with status. (Historica Canada, 2006)

In 1985, an amendment to the Indian Act, Bill-31, made changes to stop many discriminate sections of the Indian Act. The fight for the changes took ten years for Indian women to create the changes. Amendments were introduced to the *Indian Act* in 2011 in the form of Bill C-3, *An Act to promote gender equity in Indian registration by responding to the Court of Appeal for British Columbia decision in McIvor v. Canada (Registrar of Indian and Northern Affairs* ("Bill C-3").

Yet additional amendments came in 2017 in the form of Bill S-3, *An Act to amend the Indian Act in response to the Superior Court of Quebec decision in Descheneaux c. Canada (Procureur general)* ("Bill S-3").

Parliament amended the Indian Act in response to the decision of the Quebec Superior Court in Descheneaux *v. Canada (Procureur General*) (the public prosecutor-in-chief)*, 2015 QCCS 3555. The changes were created* to paragraphs 6(1)(a), (c) and (f), and subsection 6(2) of the Indian Act inoperative.

2013 Memorial for Residential School Survivors Usthahn

On August 13, 2013, the City of North Vancouver's mayor agreed to construct a monument honouring St Paul's Indian Residential School survivors. Other funds had also contributed to building the memorial. The memorial is an art piece in the form of a wave with a high point representing pre-European contact, a low point representing the residential school era, a rising tide with a canoe, and two children representing the First Nations recovering from the experience. The base is concrete, and the canoe and children carved red cedar. The monument is a Skwxwú7mesh Nation design and installation by Jason Nahanee, a residential school survivor who started attending St. Paul's Indian residential school at three years of age. He also carved the red cedar.

The monument sits on the grounds of the former covenant belonging to the Sisters of the Child Jesus. The principal of St. Thomas Aquinas High school would not allow the monument at the school where the children went. There is a 4'x 8' plaque with at least 400 names of students that attended that includes a history of the school's opening. The plaque designer is a close family member of a residential school survivor, named Shain Jackson. The Usthahn Social Society secured funding for the monument. The Indigenous Women's Studies Institute (Founded by Kultsia Barbara Wyss), The Skwxwú7mesh Nation, The Sisters of the Child Jesus, The Oblates of Mary Immaculate, and The City of North Vancouver contributed funds. The memorial, completed in June 2014, suffered vandalism graffiti in 2020, but volunteers removed the spray paint. Then a smudging ceremony was performed. (Wyss.2020) in the winter of 2021, the monument was vandalized again, and then taken down to repair this, and re-installed in the summer of 2022, with another cedar brushing ceremony.

2015

In 2015, Murray Sinclair, in his report, "Truth and Reconciliation Commission," called what happened to Canada's Indigenous population cultural genocide. (Sinclair, Chief Commissioner Truth and Reconciliation Commission. 2019.) Genocide was the focus of the missionaries, Indian Affairs and colonialists and carried on into the 21st century. The Truth and Reconciliation Commission, established by the federal government, reported in their 2015 report the following expanded description of cultural genocide.

Cultural genocide includes:

- seizure of land [with or without treaties]

- forced relocation of reserve lands for less valuable land

- the institutionalization of child neglect

- replacing existing forms of Aboriginal government with relatively powerless band councils whose decisions the Canadian government could override and whose leaders it could depose

- disempowerment of Aboriginal women through the Indian Act

- the creation of residential schools to break children's link to culture and identity

(Sinclair, Senator Murray Sinclair speaks on Truth & Reconciliation for Veritas Series, 2019)

2020 Skwxwú7mesh people today

The Skwxwú7mesh Nation has made much progress as we moved along in 2020. Our progress includes developing many programs designed to work with our children, ranging from childcare to young adults. We have lost many elders and have very few to work with our young to teach them our protocols, legends, and stories. The Nation has attempted to develop programs that will help to ensure that some youth will carry on with our teachings. In the following paragraphs, some of the plans will be outlined. This is only to show what is being organized by the current Council and administration of the Skwxwú7mesh Nation. This in no way represents what is needed by actual band members. This also does not show any honouring of the Amalgamation in distributing the resources and income of the Nation equally amongst all members as the original amalgamation intended.

The status of the Skwxwú7mesh Nation is under reconstruction of its electoral and governing structure. The band council has put forward several initiatives to change the infrastructure of Skwxwú7mesh Governing. The only problem with this is that most Skwxwú7mesh People have no idea what these changes and structures mean. The nation's resources are no longer being distributed equally or fairly. For example, all departments serve only on-reserve nation residents and actual band members registered to Skwxwú7mesh. The Membership off-reserve represents 70% of the entire Skwxwú7mesh membership. There are some services for both on and off-reserve. They involve membership and education. Most benefits are only provided to 20% of the total band population. The existing amalgamation is not being honoured to all Skwxwú7mesh. Several lawsuits speak to broken promises and harm to members through negligence and constitutional issues with the current Band council governance. The membership voted in a referendum showing 780 voting-age members – the entire membership voting-age population is 3.200. Only 24% of the Nation's voting-age population voted to change the governing structure and stop hereditary chiefs from existing. Today there are over 980 members who have signed a petition to stop this structure and return to the 16-member council and heads. This dispute is the current state of governing within the Skwxwú7mesh Nation.

Squamish Nation Programs currently offered:
The Squamish Nation has created a massive organization to provide services to around 4300 members. The departments are to serve "all Squamish people." The reality is that the services and programs have criteria which means that most members will never use a department. Members are unable to access most services. The example used is that every member is entitled to apply for a house on reserve. The housing lists are full of members unable to obtain a home for over 35 years plus on these lists. The nation only builds 15 homes a year, in categories that restrict who gets a home. The next issue is the allocation of dwellings – the Nation has only infrequently allotted from 2010 to 2021, only five years saw the building of homes. There were several years of no new building done. So only 60 houses were built during the period, and the housing list has over 2000 people and families collectively on all lists waiting for a home. This example shows how a person gets home; once you are on reserve, a member becomes eligible for other services. If members are off-reserve – they are redirected to off-reserve services offered by regular government bodies. These departments are exceptions. The nation currently employs almost 600 hundred people to provide services to less than the 4300 members who are allowed to be called Squamish and have Status registration with Indian Affairs. The majority of the 600 plus employees are non-indigenous, and most directors and managers are non-indigenous, providing services to Squamish People.

Chesha7 Mixalh Méńmen Xwemélch'stn, Mother Bear Child Development, Capilano reserve, the department works with the very young, age three months to age three years. The organization began a few years ago on the mission reserve. They are now located on Capilano reserve no. 5. Xwemelch'stn, Capilano 5, is still considered one of the largest populated reserves for Skwxwú7mesh people.

The centre could cater to up to 44 children, split into two programs with 32 spaces for children 30-months to school age and 12 spaces for children under 36 months old. The centre was an investment in the future.

It's about connecting our children, right from the earliest age, from supporting our families to come in and have their children learn our Skwxwú7mesh values and teachings and build a strong self-identity that allows them to create that foundational base around our culture so that they, along with their parents, become active members of our community to ensure that our culture, our language, and our teachings survive. The centre would also focus on development and ensure that children's gifts were harnessed and supported early.

Our children are our future, as our Elders always say, and we have to start that investment early. We have to ensure they are getting all the support they need and their families need so that they can be bright stars in the future.

When children are ready, they will graduate to Little One's School. It is available for children from kindergarten to grade three. They will learn the alphabet, math, history, and science skills. Elders come in and share the Skwxwú7mesh language, history, culture, and stories. The little ones will also learn some dances, drumming and singing, taught by elders and teachers who know the Skwxwú7mesh language. The teachings include trips to the Vancouver Aquarium, Pumpkin patch, the forests, and rivers. The children will learn to count to 10 in the Skwxwú7mesh language.

When the children are older, they can participate in the Youth Ambassadors program. The program highlights core values, which include:

Wanaxw [honour]; Nexwniwen [learning]; S7ixwa [generosity]

Iyim Skwalwen [strength of heart] The program is available to Skwxwú7mesh Nation youth, grades 8-12 (ages 14-18). The program would have been teachings that elders would have done in pre-contact times. The participants will learn to become a leader by learning to care for themselves, their friends, and their communities. They will meet once a week, to be scheduled. The program teaches critical skills like healthy communication and how to navigate conflict. They will explore the traditional Skwxwú7mesh territory and learn to help them remember to let the land heal them and find strength.

The Nation, through its Ayas Méńmen once a year, presents Camp Ayateway, which focuses on connection to our Skwxwú7mesh territory, rites of passage and ceremonial teachings.

The next group that exists now is university-age students. Seven years ago, fewer than ten fluent Skwxwú7mesh speakers lived, and that number dwindled.

In 2016, Kwi Awt Stelmexw, a non-profit organization from the Skwxwú7mesh Nation community, partnered with SFU's First Nations Languages Centre and Department of Linguistics to launch a two-year, full-time, adult immersion program in the Skwxwú7mesh language. Their goal: is to produce 15 fluent Skwxwú7mesh language speakers each year, growing the number of speakers to 157 by 2027.

All My Relations

I have written a document entitled All my relations. This paper was written in 1975 as a summary of the article.

A definite lack of Aboriginal women representations of Aboriginal women became evident through reviewing the literature describing Parks Canada's Historic Sites and Monuments. The writer verified this perception while attending workshops sponsored by the Historic Sites and Monument Board of Canada. This paper will provide perspectives on how Aboriginal women participated in their changing environment as Canada evolved as a nation; therefore, the Aboriginal women's role should be part of any commemorative monument or site depicting the history of Canada.

Introduction

The title, "All my Relations," refers to the belief held by Aboriginal people that everything in the universe has its spirit. When Europeans arrived in North America, Aboriginal men and women offered supplications to the sun, the moon, a rock, a tree, or a bird and called upon unseen forces to help with germination, birth, and healing. In this worldview, everything is interrelated and interdependent. Aboriginal women are very spiritual people who keep the language of "all my relations."

As a location in the world, Canada existed long before the arrival of Europeans and was populated by Aboriginal nations from coast to coast. Although the French and British contributed much to the development of this country during the last hundred years, the Aboriginal peoples have lived, loved, worked, hunted, fought, and died in so-called Canada from time immemorial.

The literature circulated by the Historic Sites and Monuments Board in a recent workshop I attended reveals a definite lack of recognition of the role of Aboriginal women in the history of the world we presently call Canada. Since Aboriginal women were, and are, significant participants in the evolution of Canada as a nation, their story should be told in our historic sites.

Authors Closing Notes

I have authored this book to tell our descendants about the Skwxwú7mesh people, about some of the people who fought hard, through constant adversity, to keep our land base. Also included is the story of the Skwxwú7mesh women who fought for the rights of the individuals, for example, status rights. Colonialists imposed a new way of life on our people and stripped us of our language and cultural practices. Our history was blanketed so no one would know that a people existed here before the colonials came here. This is a story of survival in the changing world that we learned to adapt to as best we could, to a cash economy, to participate in the growth of British Columbia through working in various businesses operating here. We also maintained our culture, our language and our relationship to the natural world. Skwxwú7mesh teachers tell our stories through Skwxwú7mesh Artists, singers, drummers, storytellers and other creative people.

2020 Squamish Nation still discriminates against the membership because of their membership codes. Multiple families of today's nation still struggle to get their children and grandchildren registered and membership status because of the Membership codes developed before women were allowed to vote and have a say in this governing structure. (Wyss.2020)

The history of the Skwxwú7mesh People has been written by people who are not actual families of the people. For me and my family, writing this book provides some insight into the path of history and the colonial interruption that has impacted our people for more than 150 years. This book offers insight into real family stories, and oral transmission to share one family's preservation of Skwxwú7mesh History. The use of the "Squamish or Squamish Nation:" is in reference only to the colonial-imposed government put on the Skwxwú7mesh people at a time when their rights were completed violated. The Name was one issued by the Duncan Campbell Scott government of 1923 and was the oppressive imposition of the day's government to rename indigenous peoples in their image. Today, reclaiming our people's more proper name is an act of resilience and pride to be known as the people we are. The name and spelling are anglicized with orthography as the language of our people is at a critical extinction level of language. Less than 10% of our people who know the language with any competency. This work is being done to revive our language through our children and grandchildren, and it's returning.

We are all Skwxwú7mesh, and the importance of sharing our history has been a focus of decades of research, insurgent action through land-based teachings, and shaping our legacy for future Skwxwú7mesh children. The destruction of Skwxwú7mesh is still active in the colonial assimilation process. This book offers a different insight into Skwxwú7mesh History's more indigenous worldview.

Bibliography
(n.d.).

Barman, J. (2005). *Stanley Park's Secret*. Vancouver: Harbour Publishing Inc.

Cardinal, H. (1969). *'The Unjust Society*. Winnipeg: Douglas & McIntyre.

Edwards, B. F. (2010, January). "I Have Lots of Help Behind Me, Lots of Books, To Convince You": Andrew Paull and the Value of Literacy in English. *BC Studies*, pp. 164, 7-30.

We are facing History and ourselves. (n.d.). *Stolen Lives: The Indigenous Peoples of Canada and the Indian Residential Schools*. Facing History and ourselves.

FAIFA-AIFA Feminist Alliance for International Action Canada. (2019). *Equal Status for Women in the Indian Act: the Indian Act and Bill S-3*. Ottawa: FAIFA-AIFA.

Government of Canada. (1913-1916). *Royal Commission of Aboriginal Peoples - McKenna-McBride*. Victoria: Department of Indian Affairs and Northern Development.

Gresko, J. (1990). *Dictionary of Canadian Biography, vol. 12*. Retrieved from Canadian Heritage site: http://www.biographi.ca/en/bio/durieu_paul_12E.html

Griffin, K. (2017, May 10). *Canada 150: Joe Capilano rose to prominence with a 1906 visit to King Edward in London*. Retrieved from Vancouver Sun: https://vancouversun.com/news/local-news/canada-150/canada-150-joe-capilano-rose-to-prominence-with-a-1906-visit-to-king-edward-in-london/

Hawthorn, H. B., Cairns, A. H., & Tremblay, M. A. (1966). *A survey of the contemporary Indians of Canada: a report on economic, political, educational needs and policies*. Ottawa: Ottawa, Indian Affairs Branch 1966-1967.

Heath Justice, D. (Culture and Society). Settler with Opinions. *The Conversation*, September 19, 2017.

Historica Canada. (2006, February 7). *Indian Act*. Retrieved from The Canadian Encyclopedia: https://www.thecanadianencyclopedia.ca/en/article/indian-act#:~:text=The%20Indian%20Act%20is%20the%20primary%20law%20the,also%20outlines%20governmental%20obligations%20to%20First%20Nations%20peoples.

Johnson, P. (1913). *The Legends of Vancouver*. Vancouver.

Matthews, M. (1955). *Conversations with Khahtsalano 1932-1954*. Vancouver: City Hall Vancouver.

McCardle, B. (2007, August 12). *Dan George*. Retrieved from The Canadian Encyclopedia: https://www.thecanadianencyclopedia.ca/en/article/dan-george

McIvor, S. (2021, January 22). (B. Wyss, Interviewer)

Mitchell, D. A. (1973). *The Allied Indian Tribes of British Columbia: A study in pressure group behaviour*. Vancouver: University of British Columbia.

Mitchell, D. A. (1977, August). *Allied Indian tribes of British Columbia: a study in pressure group behaviour*. Retrieved from UBC Thesis and Dissertations: https://open.library.ubc.ca/cIRcle/collections/ubctheses/831/items/1.0094337

Morell, V. (2021, February 23). The Dogs That Grew Wool and the People Who Love Them. Victoria, British Columbia, Canada.

Native WOmens Association of Canada vs. Canada, A-524-92 (Supreme Court of Canada 08 02, 1982).

Reimer, R. Y. (2003). *Squamish Nation Traditional Use of Nch'kay or the Mount Garabaldi and Brohm Ridge Area.* Vancouver: First Heritage Archeological Consulting.

Sinclair, M. (2019, September 19). Chief Commissioner Truth and Reconciliation Commission. (L. LaFlamme, Interviewer)

Sinclair, M. (2019, September 20). Senator Murray Sinclair speaks on Truth & Reconciliation for Veritas Series. (L. LaFlamme, Interviewer)

Squamish Naton. (1987). *Squamish Nation Membership Code.* North Vancouver: Squamish Nation.

Titley, B. (1986). *A Narrow Vision: Duncan Campbell Scott and the Administration of Indian Affairs in Canada.* Vancouver: UBC Press.

Verma, B. L. (1956). *The Squamish: A study of Changing Political Organization.* Vancouver: The University of British Columbia.

Wyss, B. (2020, 12). History sharing. (Y. B. wyss, Interviewer)

Wyss, C. (2018). *Cross-cultural path ins of Spirit Trail.* (c. wyss, Performer) Ted Talks, VANCOUVER, British Columbia, Canada.

Wyss, C., & Tuy'tanat. (2020, August 25). *Knowledge Keepers: Medicine Walk.* (Tuy'tanat, Performer) Youtube - Museum of Anthropology, North Vancouver, British Columbia, Canada.

wyss, y. (2016). *Ilhenayl, feast.* Vancouver: Friesen Press.

Printed in the United States
by Baker & Taylor Publisher Services